Twayne's United States Authors Series

Sylvia E. Bowman, *Editor*

INDIANA UNIVERSITY

Thomas Dixon

Thomas Dixon

THOMAS DIXON

By RAYMOND A. COOK
Valdosta State College

 **235**

Twayne Publishers, Inc.   ::   New York

Library of Congress Cataloging in Publication Data

Cook, Raymond Allen.
   Thomas Dixon.

   (Twayne's United States authors series, TUSAS 235)
   Bibliography: p. 151.
   1. Dixon, Thomas, 1864–1946.
PS3507.I93Z63   818'.5'209 [B]   73–15765
ISBN 0–8507–0206–7

To Robert W. Hays

Friend and Critic

ABOUT THE AUTHOR

Raymond A. Cook, a native of Harlem, Georgia, received the B.A. and M.A. degrees in English from the University of Georgia, and the Ph.D. in English from Emory University. He was the first person to receive that degree from Emory. He did additional graduate work at Duke University and the University of North Carolina. For eleven years he taught English at the University of Florida and Georgia State University. In 1961-62, Dr. Cook was Fulbright Lecturer in American literature at the University of Shiraz, in Iran, the first person at Georgia State University to receive a Fulbright Lectureship. In the fall of 1962, he was American Coordinator for "Operation Rovan," a world-wide project for rebuilding the town of Rovan in Iran, destroyed in the great earthquate of that year. After his return to the United States, he became president of Young Harris College. From 1966 to 1971 he was chairman of the Department of English and the Division of Humanities at Valdosta State College.

Dr. Cook is the author of numerous articles about such literary figures as John Donne, Robert Frost, Walt Whitman, Geoffrey Chaucer, and Jane Austen, and other articles treating the relationship of science and literature, and he has prepared many scholarly papers for delivery before various literary organizations. He is the author of a book of poetry entitled *This The While,* and his book *Fire From The Flint,* a first biography of Thomas Dixon, was published in 1968. Dr. Cook has recently completed a book-length critical study of Byron Herbert Reece, Georgia poet and novelist.

Preface

Sometimes a family has one remarkable member; sometimes more than one child of the family achieves wide recognition; but rarely do we find a family in which all of the children attain national prominence through their outstanding personalities and achievements. Such a family was the Dixons of North Carolina; and the *Houston Post-Dispatch*, in summarizing the careers of the family, referred to its members as "products of the South [who] were among the most brilliant contributions to the intellectual world that the South has made since the War Between the States. That [they] should attain to national fame in different realms is an interesting coincidence, and marks the Dixon family as one of the most distinguished in the country."

A. C. Dixon, the eldest child, won international acclaim as one of the greatest ministers of his day. The youngest son, Frank, by his powerful and brilliant oratory, became one of the nation's most popular figures on the lecture circuits and was for years president of the American Chautauqua Society. Addie Dixon Thacker gained wide attention as an author, and Delia Dixon Carroll was one of the most famous female physicians in the country. In yet another member of the family, however, we find the personality and ability which left a great impact upon the American public. Rarely does a man gain great success in more than one profession, and even more rarely does a man achieve fame in three or more professions; but Thomas Dixon did. Famous legislator, preacher, actor, playwright, novelist, motion-picture producer, and real-estate entrepreneur, he rose to renown and wealth, only to lose much of the fame and all of the wealth which had made his name known to millions of people. Dixon's personality was of that brilliant, complex, and colorful order which is sometimes startling in its ascent and swift in its decline. During the first two decades of the twentieth century, his wealth from the sale of his novels was such that he could indulge himself in any of the pleasures that money could buy, and his name was always before the public; yet, by 1934, he was, by his own admission, nearly penniless; and his last novel in 1939 was a failure. Dixon had ridden the swelling tide of interest in the "Reconstructed South," Socialism, women's suffrage, and World War I; and, when interest in these issues subsided, Dixon's fame also sank. The versatile and meteoric career of the man who won and lost so much renown and fortune provides one of the most colorful chapters in American letters.

Before the publication in 1968 of my *Fire From the Flint: The Amazing Careers of Thomas Dixon,* no biography of Dixon had been published. That work attempted to delineate the external aspects of Dixon's careers and personality for the general reading public. This present study is directed primarily toward the student of American literary culture. *Fire From the Flint* recounts numerous details of human interest concerning Dixon and attempts to achieve a unity of purpose by concentrating on the chronological development of the complex personality of Dixon in his various careers. This study contains a more detailed analysis of Dixon's creativity and influence. Unless the biographical facts relate directly to Dixon as a writer, they have usually been reduced or eliminated. For the reader who may not have access to *Fire From the Flint,* the present study provides, however, sufficient biographical data for him to see in general outline the life of Dixon. In view of the great diversity of Dixon's endeavors, and the fact that he was sometimes involved simultaneously in several, this study attempts to categorize each separately. For example, although Dixon wrote novels over a period of more than forty years, he was also engaged at the same time in numerous other activities; therefore, his various endeavors are categorized and discussed as separate entities.

Preface

I wish to acknowledge my debt to Valdosta State College for releasing me from my academic duties so that I could write and to my wife Mary Margaret who helped to "guard" my time so that I could complete the study.

RAYMOND A. COOK

Valdosta State College

Contents

Chronology

1864 Thomas Dixon, Jr., born in a farmhouse near Shelby, North Carolina, January 11, 1864; son of Thomas Dixon, Sr., and Amanda McAfee.

1865 The Dixon family, because of poverty, forced to give up the farm; moved into a house on the square of Shelby.

1870 Dixon's brother Frank fell, dislocating his hip. He was to walk on crutches for the remainder of his life.

1872 The Dixon family moved back to the farmhouse on Buffalo Creek about six miles from Shelby.

1874 Young Dixon became full-fledged plowhand.

1877 Entered Shelby Academy.

1879 Entered Wake Forest College.

1883 Graduated from Wake Forest in June with a master of arts degree and with the highest honors ever achieved at that institution. He also won a scholarship to The Johns Hopkins University.

1883 Entered The Johns Hopkins University in September; formed friendship with fellow-student Woodrow Wilson.

1884 Left Johns Hopkins for New York City, January 11, to enter a career in the theater.

1884   Returned to Shelby the last week of May; ran for the state legislature, and was elected.

1885   Completed law school at Greensboro, North Carolina; began to practice.

1886   Married Harriet Bussey, March 3.

1886   Ordained as a Baptist minister, October 6.

1887   Served charges in Goldsboro and Raleigh, North Carolina.

1887   Went in the fall to serve the Dudley Street Church in Boston, Massachusetts.

1888   Nominated Woodrow Wilson for an honorary doctorate at Wake Forest College.

1889   Moved in August from Boston to the Twenty-third Street Baptist Church in New York City; formed friendship with John D. Rockefeller.

1889-   Lectured widely throughout the country.
1895

1895   Resigned from the Baptist Ministry, March 11, to found a nondenominational church, "Church of the People."

1897   Acquired in the fall "Elmington Manor" at Dixondale, Virginia, on Chesapeake Bay.

1899   Resigned, January 14, from his nondenominational church to return to the Baptist ministry; did not accept another charge.

1903   Published *The Leopard's Spots.*

1904   Published *The One Woman.*

1905   Published *The Clansman.*

1905-1906 The play *The Clansman*, adapted from the novel, toured the country with unprecedented publicity and sensationalism.

1907 Lost fortune in the stock market. Published, in July, *The Traitor*.

1907-1909 Toured the country with his dramatic productions. Produced *The Sins of the Father;* published *Comrades*.

1910 Widely acclaimed as an actor.

1911 Published *The Root of Evil*.

1912 Toured England and the Continent with his wife.

1913 Met late in the year Harry E. Aitken who agreed to produce *The Clansman,* a motion picture.

1915 On February 15, Dixon and seventy-five other persons previewed *The Birth of a Nation* (the title changed from *The Clansman).* On February 18 and 19 *The Birth of a Nation* was shown to President Wilson and his cabinet, the Supreme Court, and both houses of Congress. *The Birth of a Nation* created the greatest sensation of the time. Published *The Foolish Virgin*.

1916 Premiere of *The Fall of a Nation* at the Liberty Theatre in New York City.

1918 Motion picture version of *The One Woman* produced.

1919 Published *The Way of a Man*. Son, Jordan, died March 18.

1920 Produced a drama on Abraham Lincoln, *A Man of the People*.

1923 Produced the film *The Mark of the Beast*.

1925 Published *The Love Complex.* Brother, Frank, died May 23. Brother, Clarence, died June 14. Began ambitious real-estate development in Western North Carolina known as The Mt. Mitchell Association of Arts and Sciences.

1929   Lost his fortune in the stock market crash. Published *The Sun Virgin.*

1932   Published with Harry M. Daugherty *The Inside Story of the Harding Tragedy.*

1934   Made national speaking tour to support the National Recovery Administration. Sister, Delia, died May 17.

1936   Turned against F. D. Roosevelt's administration; denounced The New Deal in speeches.

1937   Appointed clerk of the federal court at Raleigh, North Carolina, by I. M. Meekins, a Republican judge. Wife, Harriet, died December 29 after a long illness.

1939   Stricken by cerebral hemorrhage. Married Madelyn Donovan at his bedside on March 20. Published *The Flaming Sword.*

1939-   Lived as an invalid in Raleigh; died April 3, 1946.
1946

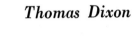

Thomas Dixon

CHAPTER 1

The Early Years

I *Family Background*

A FEW months before Thomas Dixon's birth, his mother and father had journeyed from their farm in Arkansas to Cleveland County, North Carolina. Thomas Dixon, Sr., a farmer and a Baptist preacher, had moved to Arkansas the year before. Possessing only a meager education, he had made good use of his resources. For the first half of his life he was a student of three books only—the Bible, John Bunyan's *Pilgrim's Progress*, and *Spurgeon's Sermons*. Though he read more widely during the latter half of his life, he turned exclusively to the Bible in his last days. During his long life, he established twenty churches, baptized more than six thousand converts, and was a pioneer in organizing societies for foreign missions.

Born in a two-story log house situated on the edge of the historic site of the Battle of King's Mountain, North Carolina, Dixon, Sr., had listened eagerly to the tales his mother Suzannah Hambright Dixon had told of that memorable day on October 7, 1780, when General Cornwallis' invasion was turned back at King's Mountain by the leadership of her father Colonel Frederick Hambright and his colleagues. Colonel Hambright had fled from religious and political persecution in Prussia in 1727; and, after settling in Pennsylvania, he had later moved to Virginia, and finally to King's Mountain on the line of the Carolinas, where he had built the log house in which Suzannah and her son were born. Over a hundred years after the house was erected the loopholes remained in the walls through which Colonel Hambright and some of his men had fired their rifles into Major Patrick Ferguson's British regiment.

Suzannah Hambright, the youngest of twenty-two children, married David Dixon, whose forebears had migrated to America from Northern Ireland where they had been driven by the Covenanter persecutions in Scotland. After her marriage Suzannah settled in the log house built by her father. Thomas Dixon, Sr., born there on December 24, 1820, grew up in a section greatly influenced by the religious immigrants who had come to the region. Churches founded in the King's Mountain area bear to the present time such biblical names as Ephesus, Bethesda, Zion, New Bethel, Bethlehem, Capernaum, and Corinth.

Thomas Dixon, Sr., grew up to be a serious boy of independent thought. At fourteen years of age, he had been received during a revival into the church, and soon afterward he began to preach. When the church brethren told him he should be licensed, he replied firmly that God had said nothing about requiring licenses of his spokesmen. After preaching at various churches for several years, he became the pastor of a little church on Catawba Creek near Shelby, North Carolina. Shortly afterward, when he was twenty-seven years of age, he married the thirteen-year-old Amanda Elvira McAfee, a buxom daughter of Abner McAfee, a prosperous planter and slaveholder of York County, South Carolina. Dixon's attitudes were strongly colored by the early loss of his father, and the fact that he had had to go early into the fields to help support his mother and the three younger children made him an unceasing supporter of the higher education he had been unable to obtain. Because of a conviction that his father had died of complications brought about by drinking, he was the uncompromising foe of alcohol and became its most outspoken opponent in his area. The dedication and inflexible nature of Thomas Dixon, Sr., doubtless exerted a powerful influence upon his son who, in another generation, was to speak and write so forthrightly about so many issues.

When Dixon, Sr., was thirty years old, he was very much impressed by an evangelist named Alonzo Webb who referred to himself as "The Wandering Pilgrim." Webb, a native Englishman, had come to North Carolina via Canada and the Great Lakes. Though originally a Methodist, he said his study of the original Greek Testament had given him such new light on the sacrament of baptism that he had left the Methodist Church and had become a Baptist. After hearing Webb preach at a camp meeting in Lincoln County, Dixon, Sr., invited Webb to speak in the churches which he served. Webb, a man of some learning and a student of the Greek language, conceived his main mission in life to be to educate Christendom about baptism. His argument made Dixon, Sr., yearn more than ever for the college training which had been denied him.

Unfortunately, The Wandering Pilgrim was almost a monomaniac about baptism. He never preached without discussing it, and he denounced severely all who practiced any form of baptism other than total immersion. Soon the whole area was in a turmoil, and within a short time two thousand persons left the Methodists to join the Baptists. Elder William Curtis, the president of a college for women at Limestone Springs, South Carolina, challenged Webb to a debate which resulted in Webb's being pronounced a heretic. But Dixon, Sr., continued to support Webb's right to preach. Dixon thought that, if the knowledge of one Greek word *baptizein* (to immerse completely) could give Webb so much influence, it was important for a preacher to know the whole Greek Testament. He therefore solemnly determined that no matter what the cost in sacrifice, his sons would go to college and study Greek.

When Dixon, Sr., had moved to Arkansas in 1862, he had thought that he might be able to rear his family in comparative safety from the threat of enemy occupation. Now, only a year later, the whole Confederacy seemed to be disintegrating. The Confederacy was cut in half, and Arkansas was in immediate danger of occupation by Union forces. Dixon, Sr., realized that, if he were to save his old home and his wife's inheritance, he had to return to North Carolina with all possible haste; but his doing so presented many difficulties. Though he was offered one hundred thousand dollars in gold for the slaves which his wife brought as patrimony to their marriage, he refused to sell any of them. He said that he preferred not to own slaves, and he could not bring himself to sell them to someone who might abuse them.

To avoid the hostile Union forces, the elder Dixon journeyed far to the South, crossed the northern tip of Mississippi, and proceeded through Alabama, Georgia, and the central part of South Carolina. Over the crooked roads of the time, the journey extended more than two thousand miles; more than a thousand miles of this distance lay between the fluctuating battle lines. Frequently Thomas Dixon, Sr., had to make scouting expeditions lasting several days. During his absence, his pregnant wife, Amanda, was guarded by two slaves; and, when she dozed, a rifle lay across her knees. By 1863, she had already lost three children; and her eight-year-old son Clarence was of special concern to her.[1] A few weeks earlier she had buried her second child in Arkansas; now she was desperately homesick for her people in Carolina. Dispirited by her sorrow and homesickness, she lived in constant dread that she would not reach her old home for the birth of the coming child.

When the group finally reached North Carolina, it hastened to the old Hambright home near King's Mountain where Suzannah Hambright Dixon was still living and was anxiously wondering about the fate of her son and his family. From King's Mountain the caravan moved on twelve miles to a region near Shelby, North Carolina; there Dixon's father halted, and in August, 1863, bought a farm. On January 11, 1864, during the last months of the war, Thomas Dixon, Jr., was born.

II *Life During Reconstruction*

When the Civil War was over, the Dixon family found itself nearly destitute. A constant stream of soldiers on their way home in South Carolina, Alabama, and Georgia, asked for food. At night they burned the fence rails for camp fires, and the little livestock the Dixons had wandered off and were doubtless eaten by the near-starving soldiers. The slaves who had been emancipated now returned, asking to be taken back on the old terms; but the elder Dixon sadly told them that he was unable to support them. When he had first returned to North Carolina, he had carefully buried one hundred dollars in gold in a secluded spot near his farmhouse against the day when he knew he would have nothing else. Before leaving the farm, he dug up the money, moved to an old house on the square in Shelby, and opened a little adjoining store.

Thomas Dixon, Jr., was never to forget his vivid childhood experiences during the Reconstruction era. In a land in which lawless acts were daily occurrences and in which violent enmities left over from the war were aggravated by the pressures and counter-pressures of Reconstruction, young Dixon was either to experience firsthand or to learn of vicariously through the accounts of his elders sights that affected his attitudes for the rest of his life. He said that no one who had not lived in the South during Reconstruction could understand the sense of injustice which his family and friends suffered. In our day of conflicting views about whether or not the South ultimately benefited or suffered from Reconstruction, we should remember that Thomas Dixon never swerved from the conviction that the era was one of the great tragedies of history; and he spent much of his public career attempting to tell the "true story."

Dixon's first memory of the Ku Klux Klan, which he saw as a child, was an experience he never forgot; for he witnessed an act of violence which left a powerful and lasting effect upon him. The widow of a soldier who had served under Dixon's uncle, Colonel Lee Roy McAfee,[2] came in tears one day with the story that an escaped Negro convict had raped the woman's daughter. That night, shortly after twelve o'clock, young Thomas was awakened by the pounding of horses' hooves. From his doorway, he saw the Klan, fifteen hundred strong, hang the Negro in the middle of the town square and riddle his body with bullets. The incident found its way into one of his novels many years later.

The Klan, organized at first to combat the corrupt practices of Reconstruction, before long came under the leadership of men who left on the Klan a trademark of violence for later generations. Responsible men—such as Dixon's father and his uncle, Colonel McAfee—took part in the early Klan in an effort to bring some sort of order from the chaos of the times. When these men saw that the secret nature of the Klan made it possible for irresponsible and disreputable persons to carry out deeds of violence, they tried to disband it. One day, when young Thomas Dixon and his father were met in the road by a group of swearing, drinking men who said they were on their way to beat up an "insolent nigger," Dixon's father drove their horse Bessie so hard in an effort to enlist the aid of Colonel McAfee against the men that the horse died of exhaustion as they wheeled into McAfee's yard. This incident was also later used by Dixon in a novel.

One of the bright memories from Dixon's childhood was a little Negro boy named Dick who had been brought to the Dixon household nearly dead of a brutal beating given him by his drunken father. The boys were about the same age, and they shared the games and secrets of childhood. Little Dick later disappeared after a thrashing by a local Negro preacher. Dick, using a magnifying glass, had set fire to the straw on the church benches during a sermon. Dixon recalled that a favorite loafing spot for him and Dick was under a big aspen tree in front of the Dixon store. Here the townsfolk often gathered; and, as there was not much to sell or much money with which to buy, the boys heard much talk about politics.

It was here that young Thomas had answered, when asked what he intended to be when he grew up, that he was going to be a "Gawddam Pussecuter" [prosecuting attorney], a term he had doubtless overheard; but his answer was prophetic of the fact that all of his legal cases in adulthood were for the prosecution. Here also he overheard a conversation that mortally insulted him when he and little Dick had climbed on the top of a bale of cotton near the tree and were listening to the talk of the grownups. A young man, who pretended he did not know the children were near, said in a rather loud voice: "You know, Tommie Dixon is a very tall boy to be still wearing kilts. They tell me that his name is a mistake. He is really a girl, not a boy at all."[3] Dixon later recorded that the first surge of murderous anger he had ever experienced swept over him; and, leaping from the bale of cotton, he seized a rock the size of his fist and hurled it at the speaker with all his strength. This act foreshadows Dixon's passionate nature which expressed itself so often in his adult years.

Another vivid recollection of Dixon's childhood was the news brought to Colonel McAfee that five thousand Negroes, massed on the state line, were ready to sweep into Cleveland County. Though the number had doubtless become considerably exaggerated as the news spread, Colonel McAfee gathered several hundred men and planned a defense. Dixon's father and older brother were away from home, and Thomas pictured himself as the "protector." He had a shotgun, Mrs. Dixon had a rifle, and Dick had a sword. Little Frank, born two years after Thomas, had fallen from a wagon a short time before, injuring his hip so that he walked with crutches the rest of his life; but he gave moral and oral support from the sidelines. The signal lights apparently demoralized the "invaders," for they did not appear in Shelby.

Early in 1872 a daughter was born whom the parents named Delia. Later in the year the house they occupied burned to the ground. This loss, plus the disrupted economy, made it extremely difficult for the elder Dixon to provide for his growing family. The political picture was extremely uncertain, and he realized that he must return to the farm if he and his family were to survive. Faced by the specter of starvation, Dixon, Sr., gathered his few belongings and on Christmas Eve moved his family to a farm on Buffalo Creek, about six miles from Shelby. The following year was a difficult one for the Dixons. A. C. Dixon, or Clarence as he was often called, was already at Wake Forest in keeping with his father's determination to send his sons to college. Thomas therefore found himself at nine years of age a child with heavy responsibilities, and the following year he became a full-fledged plowhand. The daily monotony of unremitting farm labor was, according to Dixon, "soul-destroying"; and he has left some strong opinions derived from his days at Buffalo Creek farm: "The thing that hurt me most on the farm was the isolation, a strange sort of separation from humanity. We got little or no mail. We scarcely opened the paper to read the news. A newspaper seemed a thing for-eign to the grim world in which we lived."[4]

After Thomas' first day of doing man's work, he wrote later of being "mortally tired" and of his inability to eat his supper with any relish:

> I crawled off to bed and it seemed to me I hadn't been asleep two hours when Hose [a white workman on the farm] called me to help feed the horses. Day was just dawning. My bones ached for more sleep. It was incredible that I had slept all night. We fed the horses and ate our breakfast by candlelight. The sun was rising in a smother of purple and scarlet tinted clouds. I was too sore at the time to care for it. No farmer ever raves over a sunrise or sun-set. It takes a town bred man to do that.[5]

> The deeper I buried my feet in the soil the clearer became my conviction that the beastly toil of it de-humanized its people. And I haven't changed my opinion in sixty years.[6]

On rare occasions, young Dixon escaped the monotony of his labors to accompany Hose on 'coon hunting trips, and one night he was introduced to the mysteries of sex when he ac-companied Hose to go "galling" at the home of a nearby tenant who had two buxom daughters. On Sundays, Thomas attended the church where his father preached at New Pros-pect, a church he had established before going to Arkansas. One morning, while waiting for the services to start, Thomas became involved in a fight with Collier Cobb, the son of another minister. The boys had been arguing over the rela-tive merits of Governor Holden and his right to send militia anywhere in the state to quell opposition to the Reconstruc-tion government. As the argument grew hotter, Thomas called Collier a liar; and, when Collier spat in Thomas' face, a rousing fight followed. The elder Dixon strictly forbade his children to fight; and, when he heard of the matter, he whipped Thomas severely. Dixon's uncompromising nature, so prominent a feature of his later years, is revealed in his reaction to the punishment: "He struck me blow after blow that cut my back with pain so awful, so strangling that it sent me into suppressed convulsions. About to scream

I thrust my fist . . . into my mouth and danced first on one foot and then on another in paroxysm after paroxysm of rage and pain."[7]

Though Dixon in later years spoke of his father with respect and admiration, the inflexibility of their personalities doubtless caused occasional unhappiness between them. Another such occasion was the cause of the family's removal from the Buffalo Creek farm back to Shelby. Dixon's grandmother Suzannah, who had come to live with them, could be as strong-willed as her son and grandson, never relinquishing an idea she held to be right. Usually, however, she was good natured and was openly devoted to her jug of whiskey and to her corncob pipe. Thomas delighted to hear her tell stories about the Revolutionary War. Late in the fall of 1875, she had sent Thomas to a local "doggery" to buy her some whiskey. Dixon's father, when he learned of the errand, was furious and proceeded to thrash Thomas energetically. Dixon recalled sixty years later that "he could have beaten me into unconsciousness before I'd have uttered a cry."[8] Grandma Dixon reacted to the whipping swiftly and with finality: she put a few clothes in a black bag, threw it over her shoulders, and without a word started walking down the dusty road to the home of Thomas' Aunt Polly, eighteen miles away at King's Mountain. Thomas was never to see his Grandma Dixon again. (She was one hundred years of age or more at the time.[9] Before her death late in 1880 she was to sit on the platform as the guest of honor as the last survivor in the region of Revolutionary War days at the centennial celebration of the Battle of King's Mountain.)

Dixon's mother Amanda was so angered over the whipping that she insisted on moving back to Shelby immediately. A house was already being built on Washington Street about a mile from the square, next to Mrs. Webber, Dixon's maternal grandmother. Amanda, who was very nervous and tired during this period, also dreaded the coming months in a farmhouse removed from medical care. At forty-three, she realized she was to have another child; worried because she had lost three of her first four children, worn by the trying experiences of Reconstruction, and ill and upset by the whipping, she insisted on moving immediately to her mother's house while theirs was being completed. On May 4, 1876, a daughter, Addie May, was born; and, for three months following her birth, Amanda Dixon was extremely ill and often out of her mind. Members of the family had to sit by her bedside around the clock to minister to her needs. Finally, one morning she looked around her with recognition; and the family rejoiced in the knowledge that she would recover. Clarence, the eldest son, who had come home from Southern Baptist Theological Seminary to help care for her, was now able to return. He had been graduated two years before from Wake Forest College with highest honors.

III   *Student Days in Shelby*

By the middle of 1876, Thomas Dixon, now twelve and a half years old, was a tall boy with coal-black hair and deep-set, sparkling eyes. He impressed and sometimes startled the people about him by the keenness of his wit and by the firmness of his statements. Fond of argument, he began to reveal those characteristics that were to mark him in adulthood as a controversial, complex personality. Up to this time, he had received only a few months of sporadic formal schooling under a Mrs. Barnard who lived three miles away at Sulphur Springs to which Dixon had walked or driven in a buggy. Now that the family was once more in Shelby, Dixon entered the Shelby Academy, where he proved to be an excellent student, and was soon progressing rapidly. Going to school was such a pleasant contrast to the back-breaking work on the Buffalo Creek farm that Dixon looked forward to each day's recitations. Quick to learn, he was eager to study mathematics, Latin, and Greek. Dixon's mother was herself an avid reader, and she encouraged Dixon's enthusiasm for learning. She named Clarence after a character from one of the English novels she loved to read, despite the disapproval her husband expressed for novels.

Dixon now entered a new phase of his life which was to give him time for reflection and study. This period he recalled with affection and pleasure:

With the passing of the Reconstruction Saturnalia peace settled over our world. Since the dawn of memory, I had lived in turmoil, upheaval, violence, riot, secret Leagues and Klans. Out of this I suddenly emerged into beauty and sunshine. I became conscious for the first time of the charm of nature in the Southland. The soft sensuous air thrilled me. The night winds bore messages of a mystic future in which I was about to enter. I took to poetry and music. It was unbelievable how happy one could be. Our home life ran smoothly. My mother was well, Delia was jolly and bright as a cricket, and Addie was growing into the most beautiful little girl I had ever seen.[10]

Young Dixon's best friend at Shelby Academy was Bob Ryburn, and the boys made a covenant of friendship written with their own blood. (In his old age Dixon still had the covenant in his possession.) The last months of the school term in 1879 were exciting for Dixon; for he had become so proficient in mathematics, geometry, Latin, and Greek that his teachers, J. A. White and Henry Sharp, said he was ready, at the age of fifteen, to start college that fall. The time was saddened, however, by the sudden death of Mollie Durham, a sixteen-year-old girl at the academy who had evoked in young Dixon the pangs of first love.

Dixon was not only an earnest student at this time, but also a young man who was sometimes perturbed about his spiritual life. His pugnacity and proud spirit occasionally got him into trouble, and he was confused and disturbed by the sermons his father preached each Sunday. The crisis came finally after an episode in which Thomas killed a dog. One of his chores was to be "manager" of the poultry yard. Something was eating the chickens, and Dixon was determined to sit up at night with a shotgun to punish the thief. In the shadows he saw a dog trying to catch a setting hen, and he opened fire and killed the animal. He noticed that the dog was pitifully emaciated from near starvation. A few days later his father asked him to attend with him a revival meeting that was beginning at New Prospect Church. The thought of attending services every day for two weeks was not very appealing at first; but, when he recalled that he would get out of considerable work and that he would be able to enjoy the fried chicken and watermelons served every day on the grounds, he thought better of the idea. Whereas Thomas had always sat with his father in the pulpit (in those days an enclosure about four and a half feet high and five feet square with a doorway), he was surprised on this occasion to hear his father ask him to sit in the congregation facing him. For the first time, Dixon was fully aware of the persuasiveness of his father's preaching: "His face shone with a marvelous faith that held me. Once I had lifted my head I couldn't take my eyes off him. He seemed to be talking intimately with God, a loving Father, and still the Almighty Ruler of the universe. His realization of God's nearness and omnipotence was awe inspiring."[11]

Though greatly moved by the sermon, Thomas Dixon had no thought that his father was trying to convert him. Dixon was in no hurry to get excited over religion; he had plenty of time to think about that while he was enjoying the delicious food and the company of the boys and girls on the church grounds. But, by the end of the first week, he was greatly affected. When his father called on sinners to repent, Thomas tried to comply; but he could not seem to think of enough he had done to be condemned to "everlasting hell" as his father had indicated. He recalled without penitence the night he had gone "galling" and had sat on the lap of the buxom girl and kissed her. He felt no guilt when he remembered that he had later lied to his father about the matter, for he construed his lie as instrumental in saving the girl's good name. But then, suddenly, he remembered the dog he had killed. In this act, he thought, he *had* sinned; and, as the image of the poor animal which had nearly starved of neglect came into his mind, tears of penitence welled into his eyes. For days afterward he mourned and was greatly disturbed, sometimes crying to himself. At last, as he later recorded, he knelt down by his bedside and whispered: "Lord Jesus, I give my life into your keeping! I had hardly spoken the words when my heart was flooded with a sense of peace and joy. The burden had gone. The world shone with the glory of God. I laughed softly to myself. I had experienced religion. It was real. Nothing more real has ever happened in my life. Nothing more real has ever happened in my life before or since that hour."[12] The first major phase of Thomas Dixon's life was at an end. He now stood upon the verge of a new world.

CHAPTER 2

College Life and After

I *Wake Forest College*

WHEN Dixon entered Wake Forest College in September, 1879, he was disappointed at the poor appearance of the buildings. In the center stood a plain, gray brick structure, four stories high. At the north end of the campus was a small, red-brick building, two stories high, which housed the library, two classrooms, and the Euzelian and Philomathesian Literary Societies. Across the campus at the south end, a building was under construction to serve as an auditorium and two classrooms. From hearing his brother Clarence speak of the college, Dixon had envisioned it to be much larger and more impressive. Nevertheless, his gregarious nature soon made him forget his disappointment, and he entered into his studies and extracurricular activities with enthusiasm. He determined to distinguish himself as a student as his brother Clarence had done. The studies which he especially enjoyed were history, language, and oratory. Significantly, the first story Dixon ever wrote concerned the organization of the Ku Klux Klan, and it was published in the college newspaper. Early in his college career he decided to pursue literature as his ultimate profession, but he said he wanted to wait until he had "lived" more before attempting serious creative work. He was, in fact, to wait for twenty years.

During his first academic year, Dixon won the Orator's Medal as the best speaker in the student body. Dixon's attractive personality and reputation as an unusually intelligent student placed him by the end of the school year at the top of his class. But so many successes, so soon achieved, seemed to lull Dixon into a sense of false security which almost disrupted his college career. In his pride, he forgot that the honors he wanted could be achieved only by great effort. During his second year, he had his heart set upon winning the Latin Medal; but, not seeing any other student who, he thought, could offer him serious competition, he passed the weeks before the examination in pleasant anticipation of the prize. On the night in June when the unanimous decision of the judges revealed that another student had won the prize, Dixon could only stumble out of the building and lie down under an oak tree for an hour in order to regain his composure.

The loss of the Latin Medal so galled Dixon's pride that he resolved to start upon a strenuous program of study the following year so that he could win the French Medal. Budgeting his time closely permitted him to devote seventeen or more hours a day to his studies including four hours of classes. He allotted only thirty minutes for each meal, and he obtained a quiet room at the end of the hall on the top floor of the dormitory. To develop his facility in French, Dixon carefully translated into English Voltaire's *Histoire de Charles XII, roi de Suède,* a volume of Madame de Staël's novel *Corinne,* and a volume of Madame de Sévigné's letters. After laying each aside for three months, he then retranslated his English versions back into French, carefully comparing his copy with the French originals. So well did Dixon learn the intricate style of Madame de Sévigné that, when a major part of the examination included her letters, he won easily. That academic year he was again at the head of his class, and he had also won two other medals. There is some indication that Dixon's new successes may have made him forget the humiliation he had suffered in losing the Latin Medal the year before, for a letter from Clarence to his wife Mollie expresses some concern: "I see from the Raleigh Observer that Willoughby Read's elocution class at Wake Forest College had a contest for a gold medal the other day, and that Tom received it. . . . Oh, that God may keep his college successes from ruining him. Frank also spoke. I would have been more delighted had he gained the medal.

It would have encouraged him so much."[1] Frank at a later date won the Orator's Medal, a distinction shared by all three of the Dixon brothers.

In Thomas Dixon's last year at Wake Forest, he became very much interested in science and in the current studies in evolution. Much reading in Charles Darwin, Thomas Huxley, and Herbert Spencer filled his mind with doubt and confusion. By the end of the school term, he had withdrawn from the church as an agnostic; for the young man to whom religion had meant so much four years ago now found himself impatient of the religious sentiments of his friends. One day he went to his teacher of Greek, Professor William Royall, to announce his views; but the teacher merely smiled gently and said, "It's a phase, my son. I passed through it. You will."[2] Dixon highly respected his teacher's opinion, but it was several years before he returned to the faith he had received at New Prospect Church.

II *Johns Hopkins and the Theater*

In the spring of 1883 Dixon obtained his master of arts degree after only four years in college and after having won the highest student honors ever achieved at Wake Forest. As a result of his record, he received a scholarship in political science to The Johns Hopkins University, where he soon came under the inspiring teaching of Herbert Adams and Richard T. Ely, two well-known professors at Johns Hopkins. At his first seminar table, on his left sat Albert Shaw of Iowa; on his right sat young Woodrow Wilson, a man who was to play an important role in Dixon's career; but Wilson was also aided in his later career in a significant way by Dixon.

When the two graduate students met, Wilson was eight years Dixon's senior. The two students soon became fast friends, and Dixon was a frequent visitor at Wilson's quarters at Mount Vernon Place. In addition to their interest in political theory, they shared an enthusiasm for the theater; and, as the term progressed, Dixon became more and more interested in the stage. Through Wilson, Dixon met the editor of the Baltimore *Mirror*, who was so impressed by Dixon's enthusiasm and knowledge of the theater that he hired Dixon to be the drama critic for the paper. As Dixon's enthusiasm grew, he felt more and more that he must go to New York and become a drama student so that he could "fire the world in Shakespearean roles."[3] His friend Wilson tried to dissuade him; but Dixon insisted and, on January 11, 1884, his twentieth birthday, he said goodbye and left Johns Hopkins.

Soon after arriving in New York, Dixon became a drama student in the Frobisher School; and he not only applied himself eagerly to his studies but saw every play which he could afford. He thought that he had made the first great step in becoming a famous actor when one Richard Foote offered him a role as the Duke of Richmond in a touring production of *Richard III.* To finance the company, the actors were required to place sums of money in trust with the manager, the amount depending upon the importance of the role. Dixon's share was three hundred dollars, a figure he hoped soon to be returned to him many times over. He applied to his father and his brother Clarence for a loan; and they, with considerable misgivings, advanced him the money. Dixon's hopes were short lived, for at Herkimer, New York, the manager disappeared with all the funds; and the disgusted members of the cast went their various ways.

With dampened spirits Dixon applied for a role to Franklin Sargent, the director of a new company. Dixon's reading of the script was sympathetic and imaginative, but his physical appearance at the time made the director highly doubtful of Dixon's success as an actor. At twenty years of age he was six feet three and a half inches tall, but he weighed only one hundred fifty pounds. Since his gaunt physique gave little hint of the commanding figure he was to possess only a few years later, the director told him that his physical appearance would make a stage career very difficult; but, noting Dixon's intelligence and sympathetic reading of the script, he suggested that Dixon devote himself to writing plays instead of acting in them. Bitterly disappointed, Dixon took the train home where he dreaded the embarrassment of facing his family and friends after what seemed to him to be a dismal failure in a chosen career.

III *Legal Career*

Shelby, North Carolina, was a long way temperamentally
and geographically from Broadway; and Dixon soon found
that he had to turn his thoughts from the theatrical world
if he were to make a living. Gradually, the sharpest edge
of his disappointment wore off; and he decided to enter the
Greensboro Law School at Greensboro, North Carolina.
Dixon again made an excellent record as a student and received his law degree in 1885 in the same class with Josephus Daniels. While Dixon was still studying law, his father
urged him to run for the state legislature, hoping that his
son would become so involved with politics that he would
forget his interest in the stage which the elder Dixon considered disreputable. Dixon was at first reluctant to try such
a venture because, since he was only twenty years old, he
thought he would have little or no chance of winning. But,
as he recalled his success as a student orator, he decided
he would see if he could use his ability to win votes. Dixon's
opponents were Captain John W. Gidney and Major Dameron, a cousin of Dixon's, who was at the time mayor of
Shelby; both men possessed considerable political experience, and Gidney had already served two terms in the legislature. Both opponents ridiculed Dixon's age and inex-
perience, and Mayor Dameron even threatened to "lick
the stuffing" out of Dixon if he didn't stop referring to him
in speeches. The fighting spirit of Dixon, his inspiring oratory, and his humorous twisting of Dameron's threats caught
the infectious enthusiasm of the crowds; and Dixon found
himself elected as a legislator by a two to one vote before
he himself was old enough to vote.

Dixon had hardly been elected as a legislator when he was
urged to run for the Speaker of the House. He was becoming
a serious threat when his leading opponent, Colonel Thomas
M. Holt, learned that Dixon was not yet twenty-one; Dixon
dropped from the running when he was told he could not be
seated even if elected. Nonetheless, the force of Dixon's
personality was felt as soon as the legislature convened; for
he introduced several successful bills which were to have
considerable significance. One was the first bill in the

South to pension Confederate veterans, and North Carolina's example was soon followed by other states. Dixon's speech introducing the veterans' pension bill had been covered by Walter Hines Page, then editor of the Raleigh *State Chronicle* and later the publisher of Dixon's most famous novels. Page's glowing account of the young legislator gave Dixon widespread publicity throughout the South.

On the afternoon that Dixon made his ringing appeal for the veterans, he was accosted on the steps of the capital by a trembling old man who solicited Dixon's help in a cause which he hoped to present to the legislature. When Dixon asked who he was, the old man looked up out of dim eyes in surprise and answered that he was W. W. Holden who had been impeached for malfeasance, removed from the office of governor, and deprived of his citizenship. After scribbling a few lines from Seneca and thrusting them into Dixon's hand, Holden added: "I'm yet a living man. Life is sweet. I ask my state to restore my citizenship. Will you help me?"[4] Dixon later recorded that he had looked long and earnestly at the old man:

He knew that I had made a sensational speech, and believed that I might win his suit if pressed with determination. But he didn't know that Colonel McAfee who had moved his impeachment was my uncle and the hero of all my boyish dreams. I was sorry for the frail, trembling figure before me until in vivid flashes I saw the scene at Rutherford County Jail and watched the procession of brave men of my race tried before courts that were obscene farces and then led to prison in Albany, New York. I shook my head and left him. The verdict was just. The future will sustain it.[5]

Another of Dixon's bills was to establish an industrial school in North Carolina. The Committee on Education approved a study of the proposal, and two years later the North Carolina College of Agriculture and Mechanic Arts was established—now North Carolina State University at Raleigh. Another bill which drew the interested attention of Grover Cleveland, then President of the United States, was to change the name of Whitaker in Cleveland County to Grover, thus perpetuating the name of the President in

Grover, Cleveland County, North Carolina. After the legislative session, Dixon was invited to Washington where he
formed a lasting friendship with the President.

In spite of Dixon's outstanding success as a young legislator,
one term was enough for him. He became disillusioned by
the corruption and maneuvering he saw, and he acquired an
outspoken contempt for the politician, referring to him as
"the prostitute of the masses."[6] He was not to enter politics again as an active participant for nearly fifty years, but
he continued to speak defiantly concerning the issues of
the day.

Dixon's law career was brief but distinguished by an
originality which he brought to the profession. He was engaged as counsel in two famous murder trials before he was
twenty-two years of age. His actions following the conviction of a defendant on trial for arson are typical of his un-
swerving adherence to a principle he held to be just. The
defendant was charged with burning a mill, and Dixon's
eloquent prosecution convicted the man and brought a
sentence of twenty years imprisonment. Dixon, however,
could take no satisfaction in a conviction which his influence
on the jury had brought about. Somehow, he felt the man to
be innocent. Dixon reviewed the whole case, and in a short
time he publicly acknowledged the error of his prosecution. He energetically petitioned for the man's release, and
within a few weeks the governor pardoned the man.

IV Marriage

Dixon's pastor during this time was the Reverend Ben V.
Bussey who interested Dixon by occasional references to
Bussey's sister Harriet whose home was in Columbus,
Georgia. When, early in 1885, Dixon learned that Dr. J. W.
Bussey, the minister's father, was planning with his family to
attend the Mardi-gras festivities in New Orleans, he decided
to go also. At the St. Charles Hotel he met Dr. Bussey and
his family. Dr. Bussey was attracted by the conversation of
Dixon, and Dixon in turn found Harriet very attractive. Dixon
began a fervent, whirlwind courtship which soon won Harriet's consent to marriage; but, when Dixon asked Dr. Bussey for permission, the father was shocked at the presumption

of this unusual young man who had known his daughter for so short a time. Dixon might be accepted as a conversationalist, but not at all as Harriet's husband. Dr. Bussey sternly forbade the marriage, and Dixon and Harriet tried unsuccessfully in the following months to weaken her father's decision. Finally, after Dixon had visited with the Busseys in Columbus, he and Harriet defied her father and eloped to Montgomery, Alabama, where they were married on March 3, 1886. Dr. Bussey, dismayed at the deed, was not reconciled to the couple for some time.

V *Spiritual Crisis*

As the months went by, Dixon became more and more dissatisfied with the legal profession. He and his wife talked many hours about his future. For extended periods, Dixon did not even go to his law office; his practice declined rapidly; and his brother Frank lost patience with Dixon's indolence. His successes seemed tasteless, and he could not now find meaning in a life that, in spite of his brilliant career as student and legislator, seemed erratic and without purpose. As Dixon reviewed the whole course of his youth, he realized that from a boy "he scarcely knew his own mind, or what he really wished to make of his life, having inherited a restless, roving disposition."[7]

During this period he visited Wilmington Beach and stood for a long time overlooking the sea. In the ceaseless, eternal motion of the waves, Dixon sensed a kinship; and he turned away with a feeling of peace he had not known in a long while: "I descended from the sand dune a different man. A light was shining in my heart that would not go out. I breathed deeply and took a new hold on life."[8] He now recalled his childhood experience at New Prospect Church, then his agnosticism at Wake Forest. Feeling that something was calling him to a different life, he went to his father to announce his decision to enter the ministry.

CHAPTER 3

Minister and Lecturer

I *The Young Controversial Preacher*

DIXON entered the ministry with a sense of consecration and with an enthusiasm which made him famous. Not long after he was ordained on October 6, 1886, he was called to a pastorate in Goldsboro, North Carolina. Six months after he had begun his pastorate at Goldsboro, he was called on April 10, 1887, to the Second Baptist Church in Raleigh. Dixon's reputation as a minister grew rapidly, and he accepted a call six months after he had gone to Raleigh to the Dudley Street Church in Boston, Massachusetts. On his first night in Boston, Dixon and his family had an experience which provides an interesting comment upon the racial philosophy later expounded in some of his novels. When the manager of the hotel in which they were staying told Dixon that the Negro nurse accompanying their infant son Tommie could not remain in the hotel, Dixon answered that the nurse was "a woman of fine intelligence and character"[1] who had stayed with the family wherever it had stopped in the past. However, when the manager was firm in his refusal, Dixon departed in great anger and found lodging in another hotel.

Not long after Dixon accepted the pastorate in Boston, he attended a lecture entitled "The Southern Problem" at the Tremont Temple. The speaker had just returned from a six weeks' study of the Southern scene, and he reported that the South was a hotbed of revolution. Dixon felt that the lecturer's report was so false that it should be contradicted; he sprang to his feet and denounced the speaker as a liar and a fool. Dixon had long felt that the South was misunderstood and maligned; and, after the speech that night, he decided that some day he must tell the world what he knew firsthand about the South. The best medium for presenting his views seemed to be a trilogy of novels modeled upon the work of the Polish writer, Henry K. Sienkiewicz. From that night forward he set himself to studying closely books about the Civil War and Reconstruction.

While holding the pastorate in Boston, Dixon was invited to make a commencement address at Wake Forest College. A prominent member of the Board of Trustees at the college praised the speaker highly and said that Dixon should be nominated to receive the honorary degree of Doctor of Divinity. Dixon dismissed this possibility, but he suddenly decided that he could nominate another person for an honorary degree, a young man who, Dixon thought, was well qualified to receive such an honor. For the next hour or two Dixon praised Woodrow Wilson to the board members; and, as a result of Dixon's nomination, Wilson was to receive an honorary degree from the college. A news reporter, who was on the campus that day and who heard Dixon's extended praise of Wilson, sent his account to the national wire services where it was given wide circulation. The publicity arising from the honorary degree was the first widespread attention given to Wilson and helped to set him on the road to national prominence. In later years the President of the United States would repay Dixon in a way that could not have been foreseen at the Wake Forest commencement exercises.

Dixon had been in Boston only a year when he was urged to accept a large church in New York City, for his reputation as an eloquent minister was now known throughout New England. The Dudley Street Church offered to double his salary if he would remain, but he had long wished to work among the masses in New York. In August, 1889, he moved to his new charge. The abrupt change from the comparative serenity of his pastorate in Boston to the turmoil of Manhattan shocked him; and he believed that his voice would be drowned in this great mass of people. With a sickening realization of the apparent impossibility of his being heard or heeded, he sank into a dejection as dark as the misgivings which had beset him about his career as a lawyer. Here there was no vitality in religion; in churches that were capable of holding hundreds of people, he was dispirited to see only a few persons in what now appeared to him to be a kind of mausoleum as he looked from the pulpit. New York seemed to be a huge spiritual gulf awaiting those persons who were foolish enough to hope that they could make the slightest ripple on its sea of indifference. Dixon realized that he must throw off the oppressiveness of his situation or leave New York entirely.

He worked upon his sermons with great care, repeating them over and over until he could say them without hesitation or repetition. He studied far into the night in an effort to give his congregations fresh, vital messages. By the time he accepted the Twenty-Third Street Church, he had acquired fluency in reading Greek, Latin, German, and French; and he searched the literatures of these languages for allusion and exposition. The local issues of the day sometimes occupied the entire sermon. Soon the young minister was attracting attention throughout the city, and his church at the corner of Twenty-Third Street and Lexington Avenue became a center of intellectual ferment. Dixon had noted that relatively few men attended the churches in the city; he appealed to them by boldly discussing local government, saloons, gambling, or whatever he felt would interest them. Soon he had nearly all of the medical students who lived nearby attending every service.

Dixon's sermons were frequently of a sensational nature. When he was charged with appealing unduly to the emotions of his audience, he replied in a letter to *The New York Times* that, if he saved souls, his methods were entirely justified. Within a few months the Twenty-Third Street Church could hold little more than a fraction of the crowds which flocked to criticize or to praise the brilliant speaker. The Young Men's Christian Association, located a block away and having a much larger auditorium, was rented for the Sunday services.

II *Plans for the Great Temple*

The meteoric popularity of Dixon came to the attention of John D. Rockefeller, who at that time was a member of the

Fifth Avenue Baptist Church. He attended one of Dixon's services, was pleased by the pulpit presence and forthrightness of the young minister, and invited Dixon and his family to dine with him. When he asked Dixon incisive questions about his ideals and his plans for the future, Dixon enthusiastically expressed his dream of building a great temple in the heart of Manhattan so that he might reach the thousands of people who thronged its streets. He said that he had dreamed of a great business building, forty stories high, with an auditorium seating several thousand people. Rockefeller was so fired by the enthusiasm of the young minister that he immediately championed Dixon's plan; and, coming straight to the point, Rockefeller asked how much such a structure would cost. Dixon thought that he would need a million dollars in cash and that the remaining cost could be paid by renting offices in the building. Rockefeller immediately promised to bear half the expenses of the project if Dixon would raise the other half.

Dixon thought that he could raise his portion of the cost in his own congregation, but he was unprepared for the fierce denominational struggle which his plan created. Other Baptist churches of the city became jealous because of the great sum of money which Rockefeller had pledged, and Dixon's strongest opposition came from the Calvary Church on West Fifty-seventh Street. This congregation had erected a large church and maintained a membership of twenty-five hundred persons. In spite of the fact that Dixon had the sympathy and encouragement of such outstanding men as Rockefeller and Charles Evans Hughes, he at last realized that, for the time being, he would have to forsake his plans to build the temple.

Dixon was bitterly disappointed by his failure. Bold in stating his opinions, he antagonized some members of his congregation, who in turn sought to weaken his efforts. He cared little for the formality of his position, and his actions were always prompted by a personal code of ethics that at times shocked the members of his church. He did not permit his profession to restrict him from speaking upon any subject which he thought needed attention.

III *Resignation from the Baptist Church*

By the beginning of 1895, Dixon felt that he could no longer remain a pastor of a denominational church. Always enthusiastic and expansive in his actions, he felt that his congregation was too cautious, too conservative; if he were to reach the masses, he must withdraw from the denomination and establish a new church founded on principles closer to his desires. His failure to build the great temple in downtown Manhattan added to Dixon's dissatisfaction. He therefore announced his resignation to his congregation on March 10, 1895.

Dixon's resignation caused consternation among his own church members as well as among the members of some of the other Baptist churches of the city. There were persons who charged that Dixon had an income of twenty thousand dollars a year, and that he wanted a still larger income. In a sermon, Dixon vehemently denied the accusation and, running his hands down his slim frame, said that it was quite evident that he was not living nearly so well as had been charged. Dixon contended that his sole desire in leaving the Baptist Church was to reach a wider audience. But Dixon left the Twenty-Third Street Baptist Church amid strong criticism as well as high praise. His action had aroused controversial battles which were to be characteristic of his future career.

After a few days of intense preparation, Dixon opened his new, nondenominational church on the first Sunday in April, 1895, in the Academy of Music, where eleven years earlier he had celebrated his twentieth birthday by hearing Adelina Patti sing. The new charge was called "The People's Church," and Dixon stressed its liberal concept of religious doctrines. Dixon's opening sermon was delivered to a large audience in the Academy of Music, which had been chosen for the services because by this time no other building could be found large enough for his congregations, and even this one proved to be entirely inadequate. His personality had an almost hypnotic effect upon his listeners, and even a reluctant newcomer to one of Dixon's sermons was greatly affected by his first sight of the minister: "He had not spoken five minutes before some instinct which I could not analyze told me that he had something to say to the world and meant to say it."[2] A minister whom Dixon later described in one of his novels is remarkably like Dixon himself: "His voice was one of great range and its direct personal tone put him in touch with every hearer. Before they knew it, his accents quivered with emotion that moved the heart. Emotional thinking was his trait. He could thrill his crowd with a sudden burst of eloquence, but he loved to use the deep vibrant subtones of his voice so charged with feeling he melted the people into tears. His face, flashing and trembling, smiling and clouding with hidden fires of passion, held every eye riveted."[3]

IV *Political Controversy*

Dixon boldly proclaimed his political views from the pulpit, and his services frequently required policemen to maintain order. On September 6, 1896, when Dixon denounced William Jennings Bryan as a presidential candidate, many members of the congregation shouted from their seats and left the building. A month later Dixon's Sunday service was again the scene of disorder when he preached on the subject entitled "The Drift Toward Anarchy." On this occasion violence was averted by a cordon of uniformed policemen. His message was greeted by a mixture of hissing and applause as the minister denounced the "Chicago Platform" of Bryan. Dixon, who paid little attention to his hecklers, continued the services while the disorder was going on.

As a result of his open condemnation of the Tammany machine and his opposition to the appointment of Joseph Koch as chairman of the Board of Excise, Dixon was arrested and released under a bond of twenty-five hundred dollars. The Sunday following his release, Dixon again denounced Tammany Hall. Charles A. Dana, who later became a friend of Dixon, attacked the minister vigorously in an editorial in *The New York Sun*. Dixon replied through a lawyer that, should his name again be libeled in the newspaper, he would sue for half a million dollars.

Not long after his arrest, Dixon became very much interested in the cause of Cuba's independence from Spain. He and Charles A. Dana, also a supporter of this cause, soon forgot their former enmity and became very close friends in the work. When Dixon spoke on the subject, he draped the stage with American and Cuban flags; and the Academy of Music became the revolutionary headquarters for the Cuban cause. He was now so popular as a speaker that he accepted many lecture engagements in addition to his regular Sunday sermons. However, the drive for Cuban independence, the fight against Tammany Hall, and the constant pressure of his sermons and lectures undermined his health. At last the breakdown came, and his doctor strongly advised him to dispense with his many activities if he expected to live. He urged Dixon to seek a home away from New York so that he might rest unmoved by the social issues which stirred his mind in the city.

V *Frequent Changes of Residence*

Dixon's years in New York as a minister were marked by frequent changes of residence. In eleven years he had moved twelve times; and, in his words, he wore out "three sets of household goods, and aided in the revival of the carpet trade. . . ."[4] Among his various residences in New York during this period was a large home at Bensonhurst on the waterfront and a home near Central Park in what he called a "nineteen-foot slit in a block of scorched mud with brownstone veneer in front."[5] The Dixons now had three children—Thomas, Louise, and Jordan; the damp, confined circumstances in which they lived caused them to be ill frequently. Jordan, the youngest, had been stricken with infantile paralysis while the family was living on Staten Island.

Dixon, upon learning that he must rest, began to look for a home outside New York City; soon he found a desirable place at Cape Charles, Virginia. The family enjoyed the new home, but Dixon's eye had been taken by another place—Elmington Manor, a thirty-five room mansion situated on the shores of Chesapeake Bay at Tidewater, Virginia, which he soon purchased. The several hundred acres of land which he bought with the house were rich in historical lore; supposedly they had been owned by the Indian maiden Pocahontas. Here Dixon and his family began a period of gracious, outdoor living which greatly improved their health. Here also Dixon, who became enthusiastic about hunting and sailing, spent long days in the woods and on the bay. His love of boats led him to build larger ones each year, until in 1897 his builder had completed the "Dixie," a beautiful sea-going, naphtha-powered yacht on which Dixon and his family often spent several days at sea.

Dixon still fulfilled his preaching and speaking engagements by commuting to New York by train each weekend. The fact that his reputation was now such that he could ask large fees for his lectures enabled him to amass a comfortable fortune. He frequently spoke in the Grand Opera House, his name now familiar to thousands of listeners. Requests came from various parts of the country asking him to lecture. Moved by a desire to reach many people over a wide geographical area, and disappointed by the failure of the People's Church to achieve fully the aims for which it had been established, Dixon resigned from his formal ministry January 14, 1899. Dixon said that he planned to return to the regular Baptist ministry, but he never accepted another charge.

VI *Religious Books*

During the strenuous speaking commitments of his New York ministry, Dixon was also engaged in writing several books about religion. Although these books were not so widely popular as the novels which came later, they are significant aids in understanding Dixon's religious thought and the social philosophy found in his novels. Most of the ideas contained in these works were first expressed in his sermons, and occasionally portions of the books allude to sermons previously delivered.

When Dixon moved to New York, he had been greatly disturbed by the indifference of the people. In his religious works he frequently denounced the apathy toward religion which he witnessed in the city; and, though he spent much of his adult life in New York, he never reconciled himself to the tempo of the great metropolis. The endless, crowded tenements depressed Dixon and caused him to forecast a dark future for the city. The gulf between great pov-

erty and great wealth aroused his indignation. He visited
the slum sections, and he bitterly denounced from the pulpit and to the newspapers the indifference of the city officials and members of the church toward conditions which
he felt were in their power to correct:

> Here are the districts where Mr. [Jacob] Riis found twelve men
> and women in one room thirteen feet square. It is in these
> districts that they sleep at five cents a spot, on the floor, on a
> table or shelf—anywhere they can find a place. It is in this dis-
> trict that children swarm like so many vermin. Mr. Riis found in
> two buildings 136 children in two dark and dingy holes.[6]

> We have been mighty on creeds, but broken down when we
> come into life. Mighty are we in exploring the Pauline faith,
> but when we came to the parable of the Good Samaritan we turned
> that over to the Catholics. . . .[7]

Dixon's praise of the Catholics at this point did not deter
him from criticism of others, especially the Catholic clergy
of Mexico who, he wrote, "united in a fatal concubinage with
a faction of unworthy Mexicans, have thrice betrayed their
country."[8]

From the beginning of his ministry, Dixon criticized de-
nominations which exalted their doctrines over those of
other church groups. Dixon said that the air of superiority
assumed in some churches was one of the fundamental
causes for the weakening of Protestantism in America. His
plans for a new, nondenominational church had grown out
of frequent debates in which he discussed church policy.
Ironically, Dixon's expressed dislike of denominational
bickerings did not prevent his being embroiled in them;
indeed, his fiery and volatile temperament was often at
odds with his idealism and led him into frequent attacks
or defenses. As a niece once said of him, "He throve on
argument."[9] The reconciliation of theory with practice was
one of the great problems of his career as a minister.

To Dixon, truth was of divine origin, wherever it might be
found. Any creed which could not endure the searchlight
of inspection was not worthy of holding followers. Only
by seeking into all the dark corners of knowledge could man

hope to learn the real nature of God. Science found a strong supporter in Dixon; he had little patience with people who objected on religious grounds to scientific investigation. All knowledge, he said, is worthy of consideration; and the efforts of man to learn all he can about the universe are according to God's plan.

Many of Dixon's sermons were devoted to attacking people who, he felt, were undermining the established moral values. Always bold in denouncing people, sometimes even quixotically so, the young minister placed himself occasionally in situations from which only an unflinching, unbending forthrightness could extricate him. He had an especial aversion for the facile agnosticism of Robert Ingersoll, and Dixon not only attacked him on many occasions but also published his attacks in *Dixon on Ingersoll: Ten Discourses Delivered in Association Hall, New York.* Dixon and Ingersoll had attacked each other in newspaper columns, and in the book Dixon expands his newspaper attacks. At the same time that Dixon was preparing his volume for the press, his brother Clarence was also condemning Ingersoll; and, in the legal skirmish which ensued, Ingersoll unsuccessfully sued the Reverend A. C. Dixon for five thousand dollars on a charge of libel.

Throughout his life, Dixon maintained a strong interest in politics, one nowhere more fully revealed than in *Dixon's Sermons, Delivered in the Grand Opera-House, 1898–1899.* The titles of most of the sermons in this volume are comparable to those in the following partial list: "The Victory of Manila," "Traitors at Washington," "A Friendly Warning to the Negro," "The Philippines—Can We Retreat," "McKinley as War President," and "Ingersollian Wind." Early in his New York ministry, Dixon had become acquainted with Theodore Roosevelt; and later, when Roosevelt ran for governor, Dixon campaigned strongly for him. In a sermon entitled "Roosevelt's Personality," he said: "In the course of fifteen years as public servant he has ever shown himself honest, patriotic, intelligent and brave as a lion."[10]

Dixon expressed strong words against drink, both in the pulpit and in his published sermons; and he depicted the saloon as "a wild beast, that still prowls with blood-stained claws and teeth along the highways of the nineteenth century."[11] Nevertheless, when the mayor of New York City announced a plan for opening the saloons on Sunday, Dixon, who maintained that wealth should have no special prerogatives, commended him, saying, "If the [private] clubs can open their bars on Sunday, they have got to open the saloons also."[12] In one of his sermons in which Dixon urges a "lofty contempt for drinkers and drinking,"[13] he tells of his first drink. When Dixon was aboard a ship and violently seasick, Dixon's friend recommended a drink for his condition; and, when the barkeeper asked "gin or whiskey?," Dixon thought that gin sounded a little less vulgar and ordered it. The results were enough to convince Dixon that he had had enough "strychnine" for a lifetime.

Dixon's books on religion are, in sum, important in foreshadowing the religious, political, and social attitudes which later appear in his novels. In these early books, as well as in the novels, there is an impassioned defense of conservative religious values. In his religious works, Dixon drew upon his wide reading in several languages for defenses of his theses; and it is somewhat surprising later to find that he makes relatively little use of such borrowings. Dixon always presents his arguments with an energetic, exciting freshness; but his style is frequently uneven. The personal charm of the man added immeasurably to the quality of the publicly delivered sermons, and much of the glow was lost when they were reduced to written form.

VII Famous Lecturer

From 1899 until 1903 Dixon lectured throughout the country. During these years he was heard by more than five million people, an unusually large number when we recall that his lecturing occurred before the day of radio. He found lecturing the easiest work he ever did. Once he had perfected his platform technique, he spoke with such ease that frequently he thought of matters far removed from the announced subject, while at the same time noting and responding to the laughter or applause of his audience. In a day when more importance was placed on oratory than now, people who heard Dixon lecture were enthusiastic about his ability as an orator. He was frequently referred to as "the best" lecturer in the country.

During one of his lecturing tours, Dixon attended a dramatization of Harriet Beecher Stowe's *Uncle Tom's Cabin.* Angered by what seemed to him to be a great injustice toward the South, he could hardly keep from leaping to his feet and denouncing the drama as false. Finally, when the performance was over, he rose with tears in his eyes and vowed bitterly that he would someday tell the "true story" of the South. The book which resulted from this experience was *The Leopard's Spots* (1903). In the three decades following the publication of this novel, he published other novels telling the Southern "story." Among them were *The Clansman* (1905), *The Traitor* (1907), *The Root of Evil* (1911), *The Fall of a Nation* (1916), and *The Flaming Sword* (1939).

CHAPTER *4*

Novelist

I *Literary Theory*

THE works of some writers may be considered apart from their lives since their philosophy of life and their principles of literary art may have sharp lines of demarcation separating them, but such a demarcation is not evident in the life and works of Thomas Dixon. When we consider his literary career in retrospect, the fusion of his social philosophy with his literary principles is immediately evident. After he had completed in 1903 *The Leopard's Spots*, his first novel, Dixon wrote: "I have made no effort to write literature. I had no ambition to shine as a literary gymnast. It has always seemed to me a waste of time to do such work. Every generation writes its own literature. My sole purpose in writing was to reach and influence with my argument the minds of millions. I had a message and I wrote it as vividly and simply as I knew how."[1]

In the words "I had a message" Dixon summarized his reasons for writing. His aim was nearly always to be pragmatically persuasive and to reach a wider and wider audience with the message with which he was currently concerned. The literary devices which could best reach and move the greatest number of persons were the only ones Dixon conceived to be valid, and he considered fiction based on "facts" to be the best type of literature. "A novel," he wrote in the Introduction to *The Flaming Sword*, "is the most vivid and accurate form in which history can be written."[2] By using historical facts as a basis for his thesis, the novelist could dramatically heighten the glory and significance of the past; and, thereby, he could make the reader more conscious and appreciative of his heritage. Because Dixon believed that the rich history of the American past had barely been touched by the novelist, he found it a vein of ore that could be drawn from for a long time.

In commenting upon the death of O. Henry, Dixon expressed his hopes for a fuller realization of the responsibility of the American historical novelist: "The novelist is yet to appear who will develop the rich field of genuine American life. I have barely touched its surface in a single village of the foothills. O. Henry had just begun his marvelous career when death called him. I have not yet recovered from the sense of personal grief his loss has brought me. I had believed this gifted son of my native state would develop into our greatest novelist-historian."[3]

Dixon's admiration of O. Henry is interesting in the light of Dixon's attitude toward fiction. Though O. Henry at death had not given much promise of becoming a true "historical" novelist, he had learned a formula for presenting human relationships in a facile, interesting manner. The treatment of human relationships appealed strongly to Dixon; he believed that, by studying the flux of society in its daily life, a writer could best reveal the most significant aspects of history. The essence of history, Dixon contended, resided in the attitudes of people and in their relationship to one another. His interest in people engaged in their significant activities probably accounts for his praise of O. Henry, whose stories dealt with the human interest of everyday happenings in modern society.

One of the most obvious features of Dixon's fiction is the use of the marvelous or coincidental, both of which tax the reader's credibility. The arrival of retribution in the nick of time and the use of sensationalism to reconcile difficult plot structure were constant temptations to the novelist. Indeed, perhaps the most serious defect in Dixon's storytelling is his too-frequent forgetfulness of the principle that, in fiction, life must be portrayed as less coincidental than in life itself, lest the reader fail to have what Samuel Coleridge calls a "willing suspension of disbelief." Though men are forced to accept coincidences in life because of the incontrovertible fact of their existence, they instinctively exclude from fiction the unbelievable, or what Nathaniel Hawthorne calls the "marvelous."

Dixon held that all forms of censorship are contrary to the principles of freedom in a democratic state, and he denounced it consistently. While still a minister in New York, he had expressed in 1886 this view in forthright terms: "I believe in a free press and a free platform. I have no fear for the widest publicity given the utterance of any infidel. If any infidel can overturn my faith it is a very weak thing."[4]

Since Dixon was conscious of the great dangers which attend censorship, he made a determined effort through the years to keep the press free. In a speech on May 14, 1924, to the American Booksellers Association in New York, he spoke to prolonged applause against censorship, and many listeners left their seats and surrounded him to shake his hand in approval. He emphasized that censorship will lead to political graft and dictatorship:

> The itch for censorship is a contagious mental disease. Once it starts it goes on. It spreads from one nosey mind to another.
> A censorship would be that of peanut politicians. It would not be an intellectual or moral censorship. It would be political. If there was a Democratic administration, we would have a Democratic board of censors. And if there was a Republican administration we would have a Republican board of censors.
> God Almighty never made a man or woman good enough, broad enough, wise enough to hold the autocratic power to place hands on the throat of an author to say, "You shall think only as I think and write only what I say shall be written."[5]

While in Hollywood in 1915–1919 as a motion-picture producer, Dixon joined his fellow producer Jesse Lasky in a fight against censorship. During the remaining years of his active career, he denounced censorship whenever he had an opportunity, even appearing before legislative bodies in an effort to stem the encroaching powers of the censor. He held that a democratic form of government can never endure the destruction of a book, for the destroying agency goes counter to the democratic principles of free speech and a free press.

In fighting against the power of the censor, Dixon by no means implied that all material was suitable for some readers. The moral standards of society had to be maintained at a high level, Dixon said; but censorship is not the medium through which these standards may be upheld. Rather, society must be guided by education; those writers responsible for tearing down the moral values could then be scorned or ignored by persons who have acquired discrimination in the choice of reading matter. In spite of his continuing fight against censorship, Dixon constantly deplored the bulk of fiction of his time: "The reading matter which is provided for this population is of the most degraded character. It is thrust under the nose of the passing crowd. It is nailed upon the bulletins in glaring colors. It is circulated among the young and foolish, the ignorant and the thoughtless, to bear its fruit of death from day to day."[6]

Dixon contended that true beauty cannot exist without morality, that "morality and beauty are in their essence, identical."[7] The writer or the artist must undertake his work with a deep sense of responsibility for the influence which his work may have. The esthete who considers himself as not governed by the laws of morality and who attempts to achieve "freedom from the restraint of all moral laws as its noble privilege is certainly baser than the lowest scavenger."[8] As a result of this view, Dixon's severest censure was hurled at the writers who claimed membership in the Realistic-Naturalistic schools. This school, he said, informed the world that the day of Romanticism had passed, that "Shakespeare and Scott and Dickens, and all those misguided, misled people who supposed they had the power to understand the secrets of the human soul had made a mistake."[9] Dixon placed much blame on the influence of Emile Zola, whom he called "the modern apostle of putrefaction."[10] When Dixon was asked in an interview what he thought of the writings of the Naturalists, he answered: " 'I think that a lot of it is unspeakably filthy. I cannot understand how the publishers print it, and I don't understand why people buy it.' "[11]

Dixon nevertheless believed the "cult of naturalism" to be a passing fad. When he spoke at Association Hall in New York on December 30, 1894, he said that, eight years before,

Zola had caught the ear of the world; but the influence of Naturalistic fiction had passed its climax and a more idealistic literature was being created. The continuing spread of Naturalism in the years following proved Dixon's assertion to be unfounded.

The writer who maintains that he must make use of everything which confronts him for the sake of making his work a true representation of life had no justification for his claim, according to Dixon. Some of the realities of life, acceptable in their proper context, could be entirely inappropriate in a book, on the screen, or in a play: "The plea of realism in this case is sheer bunk. There are many realities of life that are not fit for dramatic exhibition. Manure is a reality. It is a good thing in the right place, which is under the soil in contact with the roots of plants and flowers. Because manure is a reality is no reason why an author or producer should be allowed to cart a load of it into the theatre, dump it on the stage, put shovels in the hands of skilled actors and have them throw it into the faces of a decent audience."[12]

Dixon's view that some realities of life are not fit subjects for fiction is consistent with an event that ocurred during his ministry in New York in 1895. Stephen Crane, the young journalist, who was to become internationally famous for his novel *The Red Badge of Courage,* was impressed by Dixon's publicly expressed sympathy for the poor environmental conditions of the Bowery. Crane therefore sent an inscribed copy of *Maggie: A Girl of the Streets* to Dixon, hoping that he would give the novel and the bad conditions it depicted publicity by referring to the book in his sermons. But Dixon apparently ignored both the novel and its author, for Crane later said he had not heard a word from Dixon; and he referred to him, along with some other ministers, as "icebergs."[13]

As might be expected from Dixon's comments, he was greatly concerned about the moral quality of the modern theater. In the late 1930's, he denounced the then current low standards:

In recent years our theatre has sunk to the lowest depths of degradation in the history of the English speaking race. The stage of the eighteenth century in England, noted for its vulgarity and low standards, was a Sunday School in comparison.

We still have a few producers who believe in decency and hold ideals of art in their work. There are not many of them but they give us a few plays worth while. One of the things that has saved our stage from the ash can has been the brilliant achievements of the Theatre Guild. For their work we devoutly thank God. But they can produce [only] five or six plays a season. Broadway demands them in scores and hundreds.

The lapse into animalism which our theatre has suffered was undoubtedly begun in an attempt to imitate the degenerate work of modern Paris. In our stupid way we have gone far beyond anything ever attempted on the legitimate stage of France. I do not speak of the vicious resorts, peep-shows and can-cans concocted for American eyes. We are producing in first class theatres in New York, and inviting our boys and girls to see plays that would not be tolerated a moment by the authorities of Paris, Rome, Berlin, Moscow or London. We have sunk to lower depths than any nation of the ancient or modern world. And there are those who call this "Progress." It is. Progress down grade to the Hell in which leper trash is consumed.[14]

Dixon warned that "the soul of our nation is imperilled by such degradation of the theatre. Our civilization cannot survive such attacks on the inner life. We must return to sanity or we may die."[15]

To Dixon, much of the low moral quality in novels and in drama derived from the faulty concept that "art" is separated from life and operates under different rules. He insisted that one should condemn in art what one would reject in life; for, since art is integrated in the whole of life, it should be subject to the same principles. He said it was foolish to talk of "art for art's sake," for art always has a double aim: (1) the satisfaction of an "organic want" of the artist (the need of money), and (2) the influence he can exert on his fellow creatures:

Therefore the principles by which any other human activity, pursuing to the same end, is judged, are applicable to it—namely the principles of law and morality. We distinguish the healthy from the diseased impulse and demand that the latter be cured.

There is no reason for regarding a work of art in any light than that we view any other manifestation of individuality.

Why should I place a high value on the activity of a fellow who, with rapture describes the colors and odors of putrid carrion. The race estimates individual activities according to their utility for the whole. The work of art must be moral for its aim is to express and excite emotion. If untrue to this aim it is subject to the law of race survival. The work of art is not its own aim. It has a special organic and a social task. It is subject to the moral law. It must obey. It has claim to esteem only if it is morally beautiful and ideal. It cannot be other than natural and true. The "artistic" rabble which claims for itself a top place in the intellectual rank and freedom from the restraint of all moral laws as its noble privilege, is certainly baser than the lowest scavenger. These creatures are of absolutely no use to the commonwealth and injure true art by their productions.[16]

II   *Racial Philosophy in Dixon's Novels*

To one who has read only Dixon's novels with racial themes, it may appear strange that Dixon said he despised the degradation of slavery. In his sermons, he frequently voiced his opinion about the evil of subjecting one person to the will of another; and, in a speech in 1889 before the New England Paint and Oil Club, he specifically spoke of his aversion to slavery. After saying that the Negro and white populations of the South must be segregated, he added: "All this I say with the kindliest and tenderest feelings for the Negro race. Yes, I say it by the memories of the dear old nurse in whose arms the weary head of my childhood so often found rest, at whose feet I sat and heard the sad story of the life of a slave until I learned to hate slavery as much as I hate Hell."[17]

Dixon's hatred of slavery is consistent with his great admiration of William Lloyd Garrison, the Abolitionist. In speaking of the opposition met by the Abolitionist, Dixon wrote early in his ministry:

When William Lloyd Garrison started his crusade against slavery, circumstances were all against him and his cause. He was hooted and hissed in Boston. His very life was threatened. Yet he simply said, "Here I will take my stand. I will not extenuate.

I will not excuse. I will not retract one single inch—and I will be heard!" And he was heard! In the thunder of artillery that shook the world, he was heard! Amid the carnage of those four years of blood and death, he was heard. In the shout of four millions of slaves made freedmen in a day he was heard! He made circumstances—made and unmade the men and measures of generations.[18]

Dixon maintained that the South lifted the Negro from the "bondage of savagery into the light and strength of Christian civilization";[19] but, in spite of this opinion, he held that the ending of slavery was one of the greatest advances of mankind: "I thank God that there is not today the clang of a single slave chain on this continent. Slavery may have had its beneficent aspects, but democracy is the destiny of the race, because all men are bound together in the bonds of fraternal equality with one common father above."[20]

The last clause of Dixon's words is, however, in conflict with the later attitudes set forth in his novels. As vehemently as he denounced slavery, Dixon maintained that a fundamental difference existed between the Negroes and the whites that made full equality impossible. He quotes Lincoln in substantiating his argument that the physical difference between the races will "forever forbid them living together on terms of social and political equality."[21] The substance of Dixon's argument that full equality of the Negro and of the white man cannot exist is found in *The Leopard's Spots* in the chapter entitled "Equality with a Reservation." George Harris, the son of Eliza Harris, who escaped as a slave in *Uncle Tom's Cabin*, appears in Dixon's novel as an educated, sensitive young man who has been taken into the social life of the Honorable Everett Lowell, a champion of the Negro cause. At a great mass meeting at Cooper Union, New York, Lowell demands full social and political equality for the Negro: " 'I demand this perfect equality,' . . . 'absolutely without reservation or subterfuge, both in form and essential reality. It is the life-blood of Democracy. It is the reason of our existence. Without this we are a living lie, a stench in the nostril of God and humanity!' "[22]

Harris is so impressed by the sincerity and force of Lowell's speech that he believes that at last here is hope for his race. He long has been secretly in love with Lowell's daughter, Helen, but until now he has not dared to express his feeling openly. Emboldened by Lowell's speech, Harris now broaches the subject to Lowell. Lowell's reaction is violent and abusive:

> "I care not what your culture or your genius or your position. I do not desire, and will not permit a mixture of Negro blood in my family. The idea is nauseating, and in my daughter it would be repulsive beyond the power of words to express it!"[23]

> "One drop of your blood in my family could push it backward three thousand years in history. If you were able to win her consent, a thing unthinkable, I would do what Old Virginius did in the Roman Forum—kill her with my own hand, rather than see her sink in your arms into the black waters of a Negroid life! Now go!"[24]

In despair, Harris leaves Boston and travels over America, unsuccessfully seeking work; but every position is closed to him because he is a Negro; and, finally, he turns in desperation to a life of crime.

Dixon here attempts to demonstrate the impossibility of the Negro's achieving social equality with the white man. He implies that an essential difference in mind and body makes the two groups incompatible. Elsewhere he quotes Thomas E. Watson, the Georgia writer and politician, that " 'Education is a good thing, but it never did and never will alter the essential character of any man or race.' "[25] This statement may be ironically turned toward Dixon, for it provides an interesting commentary upon Dixon himself. In spite of his study in several languages of the great humanistic literature of the past, it seems not to have altered the basic attitude toward Negroes which he had held from childhood.

In *The Leopard's Spots* Dixon also expresses through his chief characters the belief that Negro political activity can only mean political debauchery, for the unscrupulous elements in society will invariably try to pervert the instincts of the Negro. The ignorance of the Negro throughout Reconstruction had precluded his success in political life; but, even if an intelligent, educated Negro electorate could be assumed, Dixon asserts, the Negro should still be barred from the polls, for political activity does not operate by itself; it derives its significance from the deeper meanings of society. The foundation of society rests within the family, and equality of suffrage connotes social equality; social equality implies amalgamation of the races. The last implication is so repugnant, Dixon writes, that bloodshed would result from attempts to place the two people on the same social level. If these races must not amalgamate, they must exist separately. The words of the Reverend John Durham, one of the characters of the novel, present the great problem facing America: *"In a democracy you cannot build a nation inside a nation of two antagonistic races; and therefore the future American must be either an Anglo-Saxon or a Mulatto."*[26] The minister's words, always italicized, occur several times in the course of the novel; they serve as the thematic refrain for Dixon's view of the race problem. The problem, as he sees it, can be resolved in only two ways: the Negro must submit to the superiority of the white population, or he must be entirely removed from contact with whites. In one of his sermons, entitled "A Friendly Warning to the Negro," he said: "The negro's only rational course is cultivation of the sympathy and friendship of the Southern white man. He must do this or lose the battle."[27] The only other alternative, according to Dixon, was, as has been noted, to remove the Negro from America and colonize him in Liberia. In urging this solution for the problem, Dixon wrote: .

I have for the Negro only pity and sympathy, though every large convention of Negroes since the appearance of my first historical novel on the race problem has gone out of its way to denounce me and declare my books caricatures and libels on their people. Their mistake is a national one. My books are hard reading for a Negro, and yet the Negroes, in denouncing them, are unwittingly denouncing one of their best friends.

As a friend of the Negro race I claim that he should have the opportunity for the highest, noblest, and freest development of his full, rounded manhood. He has never had this opportunity in America, either North or South, and he never can have it. The forces against him are overwhelming.[28]

Dixon's statement was immediately attacked by a Negro correspondent:

I am writing you this letter to express the attitude and feeling of ten million of your fellow citizens toward the evil propagandism of race animosity to which you have lent your great literary powers. Through the wide-spread influence of your writings you have become the chief priest of those who worship at the shrine of race hatred and wrath. This one spirit runs through all your books and published utterances, like the recurrent theme of an opera. As the general trend of your doctrine is clearly epitomized in your contribution to the *Saturday Evening Post* of August 19, I beg to consider chiefly the issues therein raised.

But when you write yourself down as "one of their best friends," you need not be surprised if we retort the refrain of the ritual: "From all such proffers of friendship, good Lord deliver us." An astronomer once tried to convince a layman, unlearned in astronomical lore, that the North Star was bigger than the moon. The unsophisticated reply was: "It might be so, but it has a mighty poor way of showing it." The reconciliation of your apparently violent attitude with your profession of friendship is, I confess, too subtle a process for the African intellect.[29]

In view of Dixon's attitude toward the Negro, it is at first puzzling to find the following statement in his writings: "Race prejudice is a terrible fact, North and South. Our Northern ancestors, when they landed in this country, fell upon their knees, and then upon the aborigines."[30] The statement is not necessarily contradictory, however. Dixon considered his view of the Negro the correct one and as not prejudiced, and the passage really is about Indians. In spite of the strong bias against equality for Negroes in his novels, Dixon was an energetic promoter of better schools and living conditions for Negroes. He deplored the ghettos in which many of them lived, and he urged the creation of suburban homes and apartments for the Negroes of New York:

Here now is an opportunity to create a big spur in the building trades. It would be a matter of selecting a suitable suburban site and then building up a new residential town, to advance the welfare and happiness of a people who have good claim on our attention. As the Negroes advance themselves it is only proper that they should have some locality in which to enjoy freedom and comfort. They are a worthy people, endowed with many lovable characteristics, kindly, patient, humorous, extremely grateful for every favor extended them, and in many ways we could all benefit by taking larger interest in them.[31]

The patronizing attitude which Dixon shows toward the Negro in this passage is not evident in his view of other minority groups; for he held Jews, Catholics, Indians, and many foreign peoples in high regard. Jews, especially, he placed at the top of the social and intellectual scale; he remarked that "the Jew is the greatest race of people God has ever created";[32] and he recalled that his father had told him about the fine qualities of the Jews. To Dixon, the attitude of some people toward Jews was motivated by jealousy of their attainments: "Our prejudice against the Jew is not because of his inferiority, but because of his genius. We are afraid of him; we Gentiles who meet him in the arena of life get licked and then make faces at him. The truth is, the Jew has achieved a noble civilization—had his poets, prophets, priests and kings when our Germanic ancestors were still in the woods cracking coconuts and hickory nuts with monkeys."[33]

Dixon also praised the Catholics for their humanitarian sense; and in an unpublished novel glorifying Turkey, he expressed great respect for the Turk "who has traditions, standards, manners and a soul of his own."[34] But, to Dixon, the modern Greeks were spoiled children, "shallow, vain, conceited, chattering about their kinship with Plato and Aristotle, though not a drop of ancient Grecian blood flows in their veins."[35]

In *The Clansman* (1905) Dixon glorified the Ku Klux Klan of the era of Reconstruction, but he saw that within its organization lay the seeds of violence and anarchy when its activities had outlived its original purpose: "The Klan was a desperate remedy evoked in a desperate crisis. The moment it began to pass into its reckless phase and a lot of loose, irresponsible men joined its ranks, the appeal to Caesar became inevitable."[36]

For the resurrected Klans of the 1920's which were characterized by brutality and by oppression of minority groups, Dixon held outspoken contempt. In 1923, at a speech delivered to the American Unity League in New York, he repeatedly excoriated the "Renegade Klan," as he called it, for its lawless acts. He asserted that ignorance of the original purpose of the Klan had caused the modern, self-appointed "judges" of society to try to place themselves under a banner that would never have accepted them as suitable members. In summarizing his views, Dixon stated his attitude toward both the Klan and the Negro: "Its persecution of the negro race under the conditions of modern life is utterly uncalled for, stupid and inhuman. If the white man is superior—as I believe he is—it is our duty as citizens of democracy to lift up and help the weaker race. The Klan assault upon the foreigner is the acme of stupidity and inhumanity. We are all foreigners except the few Indians we haven't killed."[37] In the same year as the speech to the American Unity League, Dixon commented in an interview for the Raleigh, North Carolina, *News and Observer:* "There can be but one end to a secret order of disguised men. It will grow eventually into a reign of terror which only martial law will be able to put down."[38] Although Dixon's glorification of the original Ku Klux Klan in his Reconstruction novels and in *The Birth of a Nation* frequently caused misguided persons to attempt to enlist his aid in the revived Klans, he had no patience with them and did not hesitate to denounce them in public or in private, even at occasional hazard to his personal safety.

III   *Novels on Reconstruction*

After Dixon had been angered by the dramatic presentation of *Uncle Tom's Cabin*, in which he thought the South to have been treated unfairly, he became obsessed with writing a trilogy of novels treating the Reconstruction period.

He studied the materials he had accumulated during the years and reduced them to more than a thousand pages of notes about Reconstruction history. Dixon, who had asserted that the "Southern viewpoint" had not been heretofore adequately treated in the novel, wanted to give the "true facts." Since Harriet Beecher Stowe's *Uncle Tom's Cabin* was the most famous indictment in fiction of the South, Dixon felt that the best answer to her charges would be to write a sequel but to place the emphasis upon white superiority. The first title for his book was "The Rise of Simon Legree," which was suggested by William Dean Howells' *The Rise of Silas Lapham.* Since Simon Legree was an important character in *Uncle Tom's Cabin,* Dixon thought it would be fitting to make Legree a central figure in his sequel.

Wherever Dixon was on his lecture tours—in trains, hotels, or waiting rooms—he consulted his notes and developed his story: "Deep now in the work on my first novel, the clatter and roar of trains seemed only to stimulate my imagination. The story as it developed became an obsession which no noise or even crash of an accident could disturb."[39] Because of the long period that had gone into the background preparation for the novel, Dixon completed the actual writing in a short time. Within sixty days of beginning the first chapter, he had the manuscript ready. He had finally chosen the title *The Leopard's Spots,* derived from the Biblical question (Jeremiah 13: 23) "Can the Ethiopian change his color, or the Leopard his spots?"

The first firm which Dixon considered as a publisher for his work was Doubleday, Page and Company, because his old friend, Walter Hines Page, was now a member of that publishing house. Then the thought came to Dixon that it might be embarrassing to Page to receive from him a novel which might not be acceptable. After spending several days worrying about the matter, he impulsively mailed manuscript copies not only to Page but also to another publisher. Dixon, who had had no experience as a novelist, had no way of knowing how the book might be received. He assumed that it would be at least three weeks before he could get any answer; but, before forty-eight hours had elapsed, a long telegram came from Page praising the novel and urging

Dixon to come at once to New York. His wife had not been enthusiastic about his determination to forsake his lecturing career to become a novelist; for her husband was now thirty-eight years old, and the idea of his embarking upon an entirely new career in which he might be a failure had not appealed to her as the mother of three children. However, the future of her husband as a writer now looked brighter to her.

Dixon, after immediately recalling the other manuscript, went to New York the next day where he was introduced by Page to several members of the firm. Among them was a young man who was to become an influential novelist of the Naturalistic school: "I also met Frank Norris who was associated with the house and was tremendously impressed with him. His keen mind set my own on fire. His early death was a tragic loss to the nation. He was a man of genius. I mourned the loss of his friendship."[40]

The critical responses to *The Leopard's Spots* were immediate, for rarely has a first novel been so extravagantly praised or so violently condemned since hardly any critic took a moderate view. Lilian Bell, writing in *The Saturday Evening Post*, gave the work high praise: "In *The Leopard's Spots* the hitherto silent misunderstood South has found a fiery pen and an eloquent voice lifted in dignity to its defense. The general mass of readers will condemn the book as too radical, prejudiced and highly colored. I, for one, from absolute knowledge of my facts, do not hesitate to say that the book is moderate in tone considering what might have been written."[41] One reviewer wrote that *"The Leopard's Spots . . .* is by all odds the most remarkable of the many recent successful first novels";[42] but another maintained that "it is really difficult to see any [good] purpose to be served by this novel."[43]

A number of critics noted the relationship of *The Leopard's Spots* to *Uncle Tom's Cabin*, but most of those who did so thought Dixon's book to be the more powerful work. One critic's view is representative of others: "It is the most thrilling book that has been written since the war [Civil War]. It is an epoch-making book, and a worthy successor to Uncle Tom's Cabin. It is superior in power of thought and graphic description. Unlike most other novels, it is packed with truth stranger than fiction."[44]

The question of the historical truth of the book received frequent attention; indeed, the "truth" of the story probably aroused more controversy than any other single feature of the work. Some critics said that the novel was filled with falsehoods about the South; others answered that the story was merely dramatized historical fact. Several reviewers wrote at some length regarding the verifiable historical facts treated in the novel, but others criticized it as "quasi-historical" and as highly partisan in its treatment. One critic, in an open letter to Dixon, castigated the author severely: "I have read somewhere that Max Nordau on reading 'The Leopard's Spots' [*sic*] wrote to you suggesting the awful responsibility you had assumed in stirring enmity between race and race. Your teaching subverts the foundations of law and established order. You are the high priest of lawlessness, the prophet of anarchy."[45]

The literary style of the novel was examined and found by critics to be either finished or execrable. One reviewer stated that "the love, passion and pathos sections introduced to buoy up the book as a whole, are done imperfectly, if not extraordinarily badly";[46] but another was lavish in praise: "His luxuriant imagination and sympathetic nature have given him a natural power of creating, with a few swift touches, human characters that live and love and suffer before your eyes."[47] A third source referred to the "genius" of the author and said that he had "commanded the ear of civilization."[48]

In the welter of mixed criticism that surged about his ears, Dixon was quick to defend his work. Writing from his home at Dixondale, Virginia, on July 25, 1902, he made an impassioned defense of the authenticity of the novel. He denied any effort to arouse race hatred or prejudices, and he maintained that he had the "friendliest feelings and profoundest pity"[49] for the Negro. In summarizing his defense, he wrote: "I claim the book is an authentic document, and I know it is the most important moral deed of my life. There is not a bitter or malignant sentence in it."[50]

The avowed purpose of *The Leopard's Spots* is to trace the race problem in the South and to reveal the history of the problem in North Carolina from 1885 to 1900 as typical. The primary assumption of the novel is that the "Anglo-Saxon race" is superior to the Negro race; and, as Dixon develops this thesis of superiority, he concludes that the only salvation for the two groups is white domination of the Negro or permanently separated races. He contends, through the chief characters in the novel, that the Negro has certain inherent qualities which make him incapable of high culture. The Negro portrayed in the novel is the dull-witted, malodorous stereotype of many white readers of the era. The Negro, according to Dixon, is a brute, not a citizen: a child of a degenerate race brought from darkest Africa. Old Nelse, "a black hero of the old regime," is the apotheosis of the "Yas, Sah!" type of black man who is loyal to his "marster" and contemptuous of the aspirations of "them no good niggers." The primary goal of the emancipated Negro, as portrayed by Dixon, is sexual union with any convenient white woman. The immediate popularity of the novel indicated the deep-seated fear and widespread ignorance of the Negro as a human entity.

Interwoven with the history of the race problem is a love story in which the hero, Charles Gaston, a leader in the early Ku Klux Klan, romantically courts Sallie Worth. The character of Gaston, who was modeled upon Charles B. Aycock, the governor of North Carolina at the time the novel was published, is treated with considerable skill by Dixon; and, if we could accept the fundamental assumptions of the novel, the acceptance of Gaston's view of the problem of race amalgamation becomes easy. But Charles as a child is much too good and sweet-natured to be true; as a young man, his character becomes somewhat more believable as he leaves the saccharine quality of his childhood behind. The love affair of Gaston and Sallie Worth is the most satisfying aspect of the novel, for the straightforward manliness of the hero and the girlishly modest demeanor of the heroine are delineated with considerable skill.

Simon Legree, the brutal overseer in Mrs. Stowe's *Uncle Tom's Cabin*, reappears in *The Leopard's Spots;* but in Dixon's novel he is a "champion" of the freed slaves. After inciting the Negroes to violence in their demand for full citizenship, he takes his choice of the spoils of property and money. The only educated Negro in the story is George Harris, the son of Eliza Harris, who in *Uncle Tom's Cabin* had escaped from slavery with her child and had fled across the ice-packed Ohio with bloodhounds close upon her. George Harris is a graduate of Harvard, a poet, and a scholar; and his close white friend, the Honorable Everett Lowell, is an enthusiastic spokesman for the Negro cause — until Harris asks for the hand of Lowell's daughter.

In the novel, Dixon praises the historical Ku Klux Klan, which was originally formed by six young Confederate veterans at Pulaski, Tennessee, on Christmas Eve, 1865, and which became known in 1867 as "The Invisible Empire of the South." The Klan was ostensibly formed as a white underground resistance movement against Northern and Negro dominations. The members, under cover of darkness and great secrecy, whipped and occasionally killed members of communities, black and white, whose actions provoked the displeasure of the Klan. The fact that the Klan retaliated in secret made it possible for its members to perpetrate numerous acts of personal revenge and vindictiveness. The "charter" members of the Klan are portrayed as noble, self-sacrificing saviors of the South; and "scalawag" renegades from the Klan, like one Allan McLeod, are treated with contempt by Dixon.

The Klan, under the leadership of Major Stuart Dameron, is glorified for its work in bringing order from the chaos that followed the war. Major Dameron realizes, however, that the Klan has served its purpose when its mission has been accomplished; and he orders the Klan to disband forever so that irresponsible persons may not abuse its tremendous power (Major Dameron is doubtless modeled after Dixon's uncle and childhood hero Colonel McAfee). Such abuse as Major Dameron feared is represented in the novel by a lynching under the leadership of Allan McLeod. When Charles Gaston makes a valiant effort to prevent the violence, he is beaten by the lynchers.

The literary quality of the novel is unimpressive; for clichés, triteness, sentimentality, and sensationalism abound. The characters, though interesting, are as a rule "villain" and "saint" stereotypes. The author frequently resorts to *deus ex machina* to resolve dangerous situations. Yet, with all the unevenness of plot and style, a certain verve and sweep of action hold the reader's interest. Whatever weaknesses Dixon reveals in this first novel, he creates in the reader the desire to know what happens next. The novel was a great success; for, within a short time, more than one hundred thousand copies were sold; sales eventually passed the million mark; numerous foreign translations of the work appeared; and Dixon's fame became international.

Hardly had Dixon published *The Leopard's Spots* in 1902 when he began research for the second novel of his trilogy on Reconstruction. At the same time that he was searching for materials for this new work, he was writing a novel about Socialism, a work which was to have wide popularity as the first of a trilogy about that subject. For *The Clansman,* his second novel on the Reconstruction period, Dixon sifted several thousand pamphlets and books for source material; and he also used experiences from his childhood and from the accounts of his elders to lend authenticity to his story. But, when we remember that Dixon was actually less than a year and a half old at the time of the events related in Book I of *The Clansman*, we are reminded how dependent he was on outside sources.

At last, when he felt ready to write, he worked unceasingly sixteen hours a day until, at the end of thirty days, the manuscript was completed. The storm which broke over the appearance of this novel early in 1905 was even greater than that resulting from the publication of *The Leopard's Spots,* and the historical record was again questioned. Dixon had written in *The Clansman* the first full-length fictional account of Thaddeus Stevens, the highly controversial Republican leader of the Civil War and Reconstruction periods. E. L. Shuman, who had praised the first novel highly in the *Chicago Record-Herald,* now severely criticized Dixon for his attack on Stevens through his fictional counterpart, Austin Stoneman, one of the leading characters in the novel. In a long letter, Dixon rejected Shuman's charges, citing the sources for his information about Stevens' character; but the reply which Dixon received was unexpected: Shuman

apologized in a newspaper article, acknowledging his lack
of information on the subject. Other critics did not swerve
in their denunciation of Dixon's view of Stevens. Years
after the appearance of the novel, critics were still discussing
the historical accuracy of the work; and one critic, in attempting to refute Dixon's story about Stevens, closes his
argument in the following words: "I ask all fair minded
persons whether Mr. Dixon is entitled to command confi-
dence, in fact, whether he is worthy of any credit, when it
is taken into account that he personally can have no knowledge as to the facts which he asserts. . . ."[51]

Dixon was always ready to respond to his critics. In answer
to an article in the *Charlotte* (North Carolina) *Daily Observer*
as to the accuracy of Dixon's portrayal of Stevens, Dixon
replied:

> I drew of old Thaddeus Stevens the first full length portrait in
> history. I showed him to be, what he was, the greatest and vilest
> man who ever trod the halls of the American Congress. I dare my
> critic to come out from under his cover and put his finger on a sin-
> gle word, line, sentence, paragraph, page, or chapter in "The
> Clansman" in which I have done Thad Stevens an injustice. If
> he succeeds, I will give a thousand dollars to endow a chair of
> Greek for any negro college he may name, for I take him to be a
> "missionary" to the South.[52]

The Clansman is divided into four sections, each of which
treats a locale and situation after the Civil War. In Book I,
the action centers about the hospitals in Washington, D. C.,
where thousands of wounded and sick soldiers are lying. The
main characters are introduced to the reader as they struggle
under the terrible conditions that were the aftermath of
the war. President Lincoln is pictured as a kind, sympathetic
man who is trying bravely to sustain his policies despite the
pressures upon him to have a more vindictive attitude toward
the Southern states. Thaddeus Stevens, faintly disguised as
the Honorable Austin Stoneman, is portrayed as diabolical in
his hatred of the South. Book II relates the events following
the assassination of President Lincoln and the subsequent
succession of Andrew Johnson to the Presidency. Unlike
Lincoln, Johnson is shown as weak and vacillating in policy;

and he is portrayed as surrounded by strong, malevolent persons who are determined to break him. In Book III, entitled "The Reign of Terror," the story shifts to South Carolina and the home of the Camerons. Austin Stoneman, now in very bad health, has been urged by his doctor to move to the South. He settles with his son and daughter in the little town of Piedmont, South Carolina. A romance develops between Phil Stoneman and Margaret Cameron at the same time that Elsie Stoneman and Ben Cameron are falling in love. In Dixon's passionate prose, the book also treats at considerable length the poverty, shame, and degradation suffered by the Southerners at the hands of the Negroes and unscrupulous Northerners. A young girl, Marian Lenoir, is raped by Gus, a Negro; because of her shame, she and her mother commit suicide by leaping from a cliff.

In Book IV, Dixon relates in some detail the organization of the "Invisible Empire." Martial law is declared; several thousand United States troops are sent to quell the insurrection brought about by the Ku Klux Klan; and Phil Stoneman kills a Negro who acts in a familiar manner toward Margaret Cameron. Phil's father thinks that the murder was committed by Ben Cameron, and he gleefully urges that Ben be executed. At the last moment, when Ben and Phil exchange places in the death cell, Austin Stoneman becomes almost mad with grief and fury when he learns that his own son is to be killed. The Ku Klux Klan saves Phil, however; and that night the victory of the South is complete when the Klan defeats the federal troops throughout the state.

The novel with its sticky, sugar-candy love story, is told at a breathtaking pace. Events occur so rapidly that the reader has hardly collected his senses before he is swept along into another adventure. Terrible situations which at first seem impossible of resolution are at last solved in a few sentences—as, for example, when the attacker of Marian Lenoir is identified in a few moments by Dr. Cameron's use of a microscope with which he sees the image of the Negro attacker imprinted upon the retina of the dead girl's eye. Although *The Clansman* is sometimes regarded as Dixon's best novel, it suffers from an excess of weighted polemic. The "object" of the novel is too obtrusive, and the method by which Marian Lenoir's attacker is identified taxes the reader's credibility. However, it is interesting to note how diverse evaluations of a novel may be when it treats subjects close to the passions and prejudices of men. For example, one critic stated: "It is not without its manifest purpose, but that purpose is not obtrusive. With vigorous dramatic power Dixon portrays the cruel facts of Reconstruction."[53] Another critic remarked that it was "a particularly cheap, prejudiced, socially vicious and on the whole contemptible novel of the post-war-Reconstruction period in the South."[54]

We may be prompted at this point to compare *The Clansman* with Thomas Nelson Page's *Red Rock*, published in 1898, some seven years before *The Clansman*. Long regarded as a standard fictional account of Reconstruction from the Southern viewpoint, Page's novel seems rather pale beside the sensationalism of Dixon's novel. What *Red Rock* achieves with its more moderate tone is to a large extent negated by the excessive details which make the story diffuse and lacking in thrust. It becomes easy to see why *The Clansman* was a much better "seller" than was *Red Rock*. Dixon's novel left the reader no room for compromise. Every description, action, and conversation in the novel made the Negro appear obnoxious, even when the "loyal" Negroes are described, for their actions and speech are patronizingly caricatured as actors fresh from a minstrel show. A reader who already held a strong bias against the Negro found his feelings justified and his intolerance crystallized by Dixon's satire. Furthermore, the descriptions of the white Southerner, although he is so idealized as to be hardly recognizable as being invested with flesh and blood, helped the reader to sublimate his fear of the Negro by assuming the mantle of "superiority" so often referred to in the novel, both implicitly and explicitly. On the other hand, the reader at complete odds with every principle and thrust of the novel's racial bias found himself pursuing the story in a kind of fascination of incredulity and revulsion. In short, the novel was a minor "masterpiece" at polarizing opinions already held.

A reference or so illustrates Dixon's technique to make the

chasm between the races as wide as possible. Alec, one of
the Negro polling officials in a Reconstruction election,
is described as follows:

His head was small and seemed mashed on the sides until it bulged
into a double lobe behind. Even his ears, which he had pierced
and hung with red earbobs, seemed to have crushed flat to the
side of his head. His kinked hair was wrapped in hard little rolls
close to the skull and bound tightly with dirty thread. His reced-
ing forehead was high and indicated a cunning intelligence. His
nose was broad and crushed flat against his face. His jaws were
strong and angular, mouth wide, and lips thick, curling back from
rows of solid teeth set obliquely in their blue gums. The one perfect thing about him was the size and setting of his mouth — he was
a born African orator, undoubtedly descended from a long line of
savage spell-binders, whose eloquence in the palaver houses
of the jungle had made them native leaders. His thin spindle-
shanks supported an oblong, protruding stomach, resembling
an elderly monkey's, which seemed so heavy it swayed his back
to carry it.
    The animal vivacity of his small eyes and the flexibility of his
eyebrows, which he worked up and down rapidly with every change
of countenance, expressed his eager desires.[55]

    Margaret Cameron, the symbol of Southern womanhood,
is described as Phil Stoneman sees her for the first time:

Everything about her was plain and smooth, graceful and gracious.
Her face was large—the lovely oval type—and her luxuriant hair,
parted in the middle, fell downward in two great waves. Tall, state-
ly, handsome, her dark rare Southern beauty full of subtle languor
and indolent grace, she was to Phil a revelation. The coarse black
dress that clung closely to her figure seemed alive when she moved,
vital with her beauty. The musical cadences of her voice were vibrant with feeling, sweet, tender, and homelike. And the odour of
the rose she wore pinned low on her breast he could swear was the
perfume of her breath.[56]

A novel with lines so strongly drawn as those in the above
descriptions could only provoke much controversy—and
many sales.

The Traitor (1907), Dixon's third novel in his trilogy about Reconstruction, is a book of somewhat more subdued tone. Of the three novels, *The Traitor* is the least biased; indeed, Dixon appears to be attempting a reconciliation between tween opposing factions. Although *The Traitor* received some adverse criticism, its reception was more uniformly favorable than had been that of *The Leopard's Spots* or *The Clansman*. Like the other two novels in the trilogy, *The Traitor* had an enormous popularity. It sold more than fifty thousand copies in advance of its publication; and its ultimate sales reached a million copies.

The novel opens with General Nathan Bedford Forest's order for the dissolution of the Klan, and the scene is set in the atmosphere of the fierce neighborhood feuds which marked the Klan's downfall in the Piedmont region of the South. The time covered is only two years, 1870–72; and this novel is, in some respects, the best of the trilogy because events develop more logically and because the movement of the story proceeds more naturally than in the previous novels. The characters are also more "alive" than those in the first two books of the trilogy. John Graham, the hero of *The Traitor*, impresses the reader as a more believable hero than do George Gaston and Ben Cameron. Dixon takes a more realistic view of his characters; for example, Graham drinks whiskey, or more explicitly, he gets completely drunk. As the leader of the Ku Klux Klan, he is finally caught and sentenced to five years in jail. Stella Butler, his sweetheart, is an interesting, authentic character; she has tantrums of temper, uncontrollable feelings of jealousy—all the dissimulations of a spoiled, superficial young woman. Her childish peeves are finally transmuted into serious womanhood by the brutality of her father's murder.

This novel achieves a certain effectiveness with its title. John Graham disbands the Klan when he realizes that it will become oppressive and too powerful, and he intends to fight "to the death" any man who attempts to reorganize it. Graham was called a "traitor" by many persons when he ordered the Klan dissolved; on the other hand, Steve Hoyle, Graham's enemy, betrays the secrets of the Klan to the authorities and thereby becomes a "traitor." In short, the title achieves a kind of double meaning which enhances considerably the force and effect of the novel.

In 1924, seventeen years after the publication of the last novel in the "Reconstruction Trilogy," Dixon turned again to the Reconstruction period in *The Black Hood*, a sequel to *The Traitor*. In the "Author's Note" which prefaces the story, Dixon writes that *The Black Hood* is based in part upon the events related in *The Traitor*, with a different interpretation by him of those events learned through the passage of years. But, when the two novels are considered together, they appear quite similar in plot and treatment; whole chapters progress in parallel fashion, sometimes almost word for word. The theme of *The Black Hood* is the resurgence of the disbanded Ku Klux Klan under the banner of unscrupulous persons who call the organization "The Black Hood." Dixon was strongly opposed to the revived Klans of the 1920's, and this novel appears to have been written as a lesson to persons who attempt to violate constituted authority. The hero of *The Black Hood* finally realizes that the best uniform a man can wear is that of the army of the United States, not the disguise of a secret order. The novel, though inferior to *The Traitor*, received favorable reviews.[57]

A formula applies to the entire trilogy: the same obstacles are overcome by the same generous, brave stereotypes. In each novel, the hero, in order to win his sweetheart, must overcome the objections of a stern father. Each hero is a spokesman and leader of the Ku Klux Klan; each is a lawyer who aspires to high office in the state. All three of the novels are laid largely in the Piedmont region of the Carolinas, and each novel focuses its attention on the inhabitants of small towns. The Northerner who sympathizes with the South is treated sympathetically, but those who champion the Negro cause are invariably treated as "scalawags" or "carpetbaggers."

There is too much sameness about these novels to hold the reader's continued interest. Read separately, they draw the reader along by the sheer force and intensity of their stories; but the adventures begin to pall as they repeat themselves. The characters of these novels are "flat," with the possible exception of Stella Butler in *The Traitor*, who is at last made to realize her frivolity by the tragic death of her father. Dixon's method is hard-hitting, sensational, and uncompromising; it becomes easy to understand the reasons for the great popularity of these swiftly moving stories dealing with problems very close to people who had experienced the Civil War and Reconstruction; and thousands of persons who had experienced Reconstruction were still alive when the trilogy of novels was published. Dixon's literary skill in evoking old memories and deep-seated prejudices made the novelist a respected spokesman—a champion who could speak for people who held bitter resentments, real or imagined, from one of the most controversial periods in American history.

Younger generations in the South who had not been alive during the period of the Civil War and Reconstruction had nevertheless heard much from their parents or grandparents and had formed a strong bias against "Yankees" who, they thought, were mainly responsible for the problems of Reconstruction. We must not forget that, at the time of the publication of the trilogy, the Dunning School of Reconstruction theory was in vogue which held that the South was sorely oppressed during this period. Only in more recent times have the Revisionists and Neo-Revisionists, who stress the constructive features of Reconstruction, helped to change prevailing opinion toward a different view. Indeed, under the influence of the Neo-Revisionists, the Reconstruction era is often pictured as the most glorious period of American history, a view probably as far from the realities as the Dunning School had been with its opposite orientation.

An interesting mixture of realism and romance in these novels accounts for their enormous popularity. In the action scenes, in some of the conversations, and in the frequent use of historical dates and place names, Dixon achieves a verisimilitude which fascinated many readers and caused them to feel that the scenes before them were based in fact. Dixon perhaps strays farthest from the day-by-day realities of the life that he portrays when he writes of racial matters and the romantic attachments in his novels. Oddly enough, his appeal to prejudice and his exaggerated perfection of womanhood provided many readers with an escape from the very realities which existed. Dixon seems to be skillful in externals—in those matters which the eye sees and the ear hears; but of the inner realities of Negro life or the motives and drives beneath the surfaces of social mores, he relates very little.

Henry Watterson, long-time editor of the Louisville *Courier-Journal* and an aggressive proponent of "home rule" for the Southern states, had been instrumental in laying the groundwork for acceptance of the idea nationally. Prior to Dixon's first novels, the writings of James Lane Allen, Thomas Nelson Page, and Joel Chandler Harris had attempted a new type of Cavalier literature which did not alienate the North as had the stories of ante-bellum Southern writers. The great popularity of Dixon's novels in the North, as well as in the South, is indicative of his skillful presentation of "home rule" by appealing to Southerners while, at the same time, not unnecessarily offending Northerners.

In addition to the mass appeal engendered by sheer adventure and themes treating violence and sexual fear, the widespread popularity of Dixon's novels in the North can be accounted for in the following ways: (1) Abraham Lincoln is treated as a symbol of wisdom and national unity; (2) interregional romance (as in the case of the Northern Stonemans and Southern Camerons in *The Clansman*) is endorsed by Dixon as a bridge to reconciliation; (3) Dixon is careful to distinguish between brutal, unscrupulous "Northern Radicals" like Thaddeus Stevens and ordinarily decent Northern people. Therefore, by blurring certain sectional differences, and by not glorifying the South at the expense of the North, Dixon appealed to an unprecedented national popularity among readers of novels dealing with the Reconstruction period.

Dixon, under the guise of an appealing love story of the "moonlight and roses" variety, championed the idealized and often mythologized "lost causes" of the South, especially those romantic fantasies which encouraged the idea that nobility of sentiment, graciousness of living, and the sacredness of property were principles exclusively Southern. These attitudes, which had been widely inculcated in the

South since the Civil War, had a powerful appeal to, and reinforcement among, hundreds of thousands of Southern readers.

IV *Novels about Civil War Heroes*

Dixon's interest in the leaders of the Civil War is revealed in three novels in which Robert E. Lee, Jefferson Davis, and Abraham Lincoln are leading characters. *The Man in Gray* (1921) is an historical romance dealing with Lee and his followers from the beginning of the war until Lee's surrender at Appomattox. Considerable attention is given to Sheridan, J. E. B. Stuart, Robert Toombs, Mrs. Lee, and Custis and Mary Lee. The portrait of Lee is a highly idealized one, and a more historically profitable account of the period with which the novel deals may be derived from documented histories of the war.

The whole span of Jefferson Davis' life is told in *The Victim* (1914). The prologue of the novel tells of Davis as a little boy in Mississippi and of his schooling in the Catholic monastery at Springfield, Kentucky. The prologue ends with the romance and marriage of Davis and Sarah Taylor, the daughter of Colonel Zachary Taylor. The novel traces the stormy debates raging in Congress prior to the complete division of the Union. Through all this period, Jennie Barton, daughter of The Honorable Roger Barton, a Secessionist, is the belle of Washington who engages in various flirtations with the young men of the city and especially with Dick Welford, a young Southerner.

However, the love interest in the novel centers on Jennie Barton and Henried Socola, secretary to the minister from Sardinia. Socola is a secret agent working for the Northern cause, but love finally surmounts the political differences between the lovers. Socola is an interesting character who is surprisingly treated by Dixon with little bias, in spite of the fact that Socola is a Northern figure. Soon the scene shifts to Richmond where the Southern leaders are rapidly preparing for war. The novel indicates considerable historical research on Dixon's part, especially into matters relating to Davis and the generals of the Confederacy. Joseph E. Johnston is described as a "master of retreat" and as one of the main causes for the defeat of the South. The gradual physical decline of Davis and his final flight from Richmond into Georgia are effectively narrated.

As a life-long admirer of Abraham Lincoln, Dixon praises him in several novels. In *The Southerner* (1913), the story of what Dixon calls the "real Lincoln," the author shows for his hero a curious and fervid admiration usually reserved for Southern leaders. He makes much of the fact that Lincoln was born in the South, and he considers the cast of Lincoln's character and thought to be peculiarly "Southern." As in *The Victim,* Dixon begins the novel with the childhood of the subject as prefatory to the story proper; and Lincoln's promise to his dying mother to live a life of high purpose is dramatically, if not altogether convincingly, told. Lincoln is portrayed as a man of infinite patience who gradually sinks under the burden of criticism, opposition, and sadness. The novel closes as the curtains of the Ford Theater are drawn after the assassination of the President. The personal relationships of Lincoln, John Hay, George B. McClellan, and W. T. Sherman occupy a considerable part of the story. A rather artificially contrived romantic interest centers about Betty Winter and John and Ned Vaughan, brothers who are on opposite sides of the conflict. In summary, the figure of Lincoln as presented by Dixon is essentially that given by most favorable biographers.

V   *Trilogy on Socialism*

In addition to his novels treating the issues of the Civil War and the racial problems of Reconstruction, Dixon was vitally concerned with certain other social issues of his day: Socialism, Communism, and "the emancipated woman." Dixon had little patience with a social order based upon any collective or governmental control of property and distribution of goods. This attitude had been shown in his extreme individualism as a lawyer and minister and in his famous lectures "Backbone" and "The Fool."

We can best understand Dixon's attitudes toward social issues if we view the backgrounds to his novels. After the Civil War and Reconstruction, farmers, particularly in the South and in the Middle West, became more and more dissatisfied with their sinking economic status. The increasing productivity of machinery and the improved methods of transporting goods by railway forced American producers to compete more stringently for business with world markets. Farmers, however, tended to place most of the blame on the railways, on high interest rates, and on the excessive profits of the middle man. Out of these dissatisfactions grew various groups which emphasized one aspect of their plight or another. There were the Grangers, who pressed the railways for changes in tariffs; the Greenbackers and Free Silverites, who concentrated on money reform; and the various farmers' alliances who hoped to bolster their status by mutual cooperation in economic and political matters.

By the late 1880's and early 1890's, the condition of farmers in the South and Middle West had sunk to an alarming level; and, in the Far West, the silver miners were angry over the continuance of the single-gold standard, which brought about a drastic drop in the price of silver. Out of these disturbing economic situations arose a coalition which came to be known as the Populist, or People's, party. After numerous beginnings at the state level, the Populist party held its national convention at Cincinnati, Ohio, on May 19, 1891. The candidates selected, James B. Weaver of Iowa and James G. Field of Virginia, received a total of twenty-two electoral votes and over a million popular votes in the ensuing national elections. In 1896, the Democrats nominated William Jennings Bryan of Nebraska, a free silverite, on a Populist platform. The Populists, faced with the dilemma of loyalty to their principles or their party, compromised by nominating Bryan for president and Thomas E. Watson of Georgia for vice-president. The Democrats meanwhile nominated Arthur Sewall; and, in the ensuing confusion over two candidates for vice-president, plus other factors, the Republicans easily won with William McKinley and Garret A. Hobart as their presidential and vice-presidential choices, respectively.

Adding to the influence of the Populists was the influence of the Bellamyites, named after the prime mover of their group. Edward Bellamy, a free-lance writer and journalist, had become very much concerned over the plight of the urban poor after a visit to Germany when he was eighteen years old. His most famous book *Looking Backward* (1888) described a Socialist Utopia that stressed cooperation and brotherhood; and it had an immediate appeal to a public suffering from the economic depression of 1883. Bellamy strove for nationalization of public services, and under his book's influence Nationalist clubs proliferated. His magazine the *New Nation,* as well as some of his disciples, was instrumental in getting a number of principles written into the Populist platform of 1892.

An interesting paradox in Dixon's often contradictory nature is that, although he was born into a poor farming family which might have been exploited by "outsiders," he was never the champion of the poor farmer and had little sympathy for the Populist movement and the Socialist reforms of Bellamy. Dixon said he had experienced more than enough of governmental control during Reconstruction and after. In addition, his strong individuality and his unceasing struggles for personal accomplishment made him cautious about turning over the direction of his life to a cooperative, Socialist enterprise.

Dixon was very adept at making Socialist theory appear in a ridiculous or contemptible light; and this skill is nowhere better shown than in *The One Woman,* published in 1903 as the first of a trilogy of novels about Socialism. This novel contains a plot that stems from Dixon's personal experience. The experience in question occurred early in Dixon's ministry in New York when a charming young woman in the congregation had come to him to say that she had fallen in love with him. After Dixon had tried to extricate himself from the delicate situation as well as he could, the woman, a writer, had transmuted the experience into a story which had been published in a popular magazine; and this situation is quite likely the basis for *The One Woman* since such a confession occurs in the novel. There are other autobiographical hints, for the personality of the leading character Frank Gordon is very similar to that of Dixon. In addition, Gordon's desire to establish a new independent church parallels Dixon's attempt to do the same.[58]

In the novel, Gordon, a dynamic minister with Socialist

leanings, is gradually drawn from his family by the charming and wealthy Kate Ransom. At last he divorces his wife and marries Kate who has given a million dollars toward his new, independent church. Dixon gives an ironic twist to what he considered the Socialist evil of "shared wealth" by having Gordon's best friend fall in love with Gordon's new wife. When Kate leaves him, Gordon kills his old friend Mark Overman and is twice sentenced to death. At the last moment he is spared by Morris King, the governor of New York, who was an old sweetheart of Gordon's first wife Ruth.

Dixon portrays Gordon as an unsophisticated, idealistic dreamer who sees society as a group of innocent children who will instinctively turn to good if but shown the way. He is the outspoken champion of the masses who fights the capitalistic monopolies which perpetuate the bad working conditions of the poor. Unfortunately, as Dixon delineates him, Gordon lacks the pragmatic insight of his cynical friend Mark Overman who foresees the inevitable result of unharnessed restraint. Moreover, all the issues of the story are resolved at the close of the novel, despite the fact that they seem impossible of resolution within a few pages of the end. This wrenching of probabilities and the intensely emotional quality of Dixon's thesis are the weakest features of the novel, but portions of the story have great moral persuasiveness and show sincerity of purpose. Dixon, as he frequently does, pictures the people and events on a grand scale. All the characters are prominent in New York society, and their actions influence the lives of thousands of people. By effectively showing the gradual disintegration of character in those who attempt to discard the shackles of convention, Dixon makes a strong case against what he construed to be one aspect of the "socialistic evil."

The One Woman, which was Dixon's second novel, was as eagerly read by the public as *The Leopard's Spots* had been. A critic who reviewed Dixon's novel—along with other new ones by James Lane Allen, Thomas Nelson Page, Jack London, and John Fox, Jr.—said in part that "Every color in it is flamboyant, and every sound a scream. But it is powerful with elementary force and the passages describing the life of a city preacher carry weight by a sense of personal experience."[59]

When Dixon submitted *The One Woman* to Doubleday, Page, and Company, he was told to name his own scale of royalties—a response that most authors only dream about. The fact that Dixon had again written a best-seller is indicated by the following evaluation:

> It is doubtful if any book of the year has excited quite the amount of controversy that has been accorded "The One Woman." It murders Socialism with the same animalism with which the hero kills his friend. It paints in colors that are not to be mistaken the consequences of the too common social evil. The action is terrifically and breathlessly rapid. You will read it over and over in whole or piecemeal. You will be enraptured and angered. You will think about it and dream about it. You will praise it and condemn it, admire and despise it. And after all you decide that it is a great book.[60]

The publishers said of the novel that "no book published in recent times has received such a torrent of savage abuse from unknown critics, and such enthusiastic praise from the leaders of thought."[61]

Comrades (1909), the second novel of the trilogy, is a story of an attempt to establish a Socialist state on an island off the California coast. The difficulties encountered in the effort to try to force humanity into following impossible and inconsistent ideals emphasize in sharp satirical lines Dixon's social creed. The novel reveals, however, few principles of Socialist thought; instead, the story is developed by playing the personalities of the characters against one another. The more ludicrous features of the Socialist experiment are effectively derided by Dixon; the chapter "A Call for Heroes" is a good case in point.

The characters of the novel include Norman Worth, an amateur Socialist of high ideals; Barbara Bozenta, "a new Joan of Arc" who is the sweetheart of Norman; Colonel Worth, a firm capitalist; Herman and Catherine Wolf, the malignant forces in the experimental colony; and a number of minor figures. Norman Worth is treated as a well-meaning but sadly misdirected young man. He is finally made to see the truth in his father's warnings about Socialism as the colony rises in revolt and as Norman and Barbara barely escape with their lives. The day is saved at last by a detachment of United States troops who suppress the uprising; and, as the red flag of Socialism is hauled down and the American flag is hoisted in its place, Norman belatedly remarks to his father that the American flag is really beautiful after all.

In this novel Dixon attempts to demonstrate that it is impossible for people of all classes and degrees of attainment to be completely leveled as a social group. In the colony of only a few hundred persons, there are scores of would-be "preachers," "actresses," and "writers." Since most of the members of the colony have chosen the more "glamorous" jobs, no one is left to do the domestic work. A new élite arises among the cleaning women, and they demand so much for their services that they soon become the highest paid workers of the colony. In an effort to meet everyone's demands, the working day is eventually reduced to two hours. Such a society as Dixon pictures is doomed to fall; and in this caricature of the unattractive features of Socialism the author makes his book interesting satire.

In *The Root of Evil* (1911), the last in the trilogy of novels about Socialism, Dixon departs considerably from the theme of the first two books; for only indirectly is he concerned with Socialism: the novel is more a refutation of extreme capitalistic principles than a sermon against Socialism. Dixon's argument is that the salvation of society lies in the "golden mean" between the extremes of "capitalistic greed" and "socialistic idealism." Mr. Bivens represents the uncompromising, greedy capitalist; Dr. Woodman is pictured as the misdirected idealist who, through his persistent philosophy of shared wealth, finally loses everything and is reduced to thievery in order to support his daughter. Torn between these extremes of character is James Stuart, a young man who is almost destroyed in the tug-of-war which goes on: shall he join the unscrupulous Mr. Bivens in business, ignoring the system of ethics in which he was reared; or shall he maintain his idealism and sink into desperation as did Dr. Woodman? Nan Primrose, Stuart's sweetheart, insists that he join Mr. Bivens and thereby become wealthy. Stuart is sickened by the animalism of Bivens; finally he sees that his road runs in another direction. His decision costs him his sweetheart, but he is enriched immeasurably by the sense of peace and self-respect which return with the victory of his ethical principles.

Through all the novels of the trilogy on Socialism, Dixon wove an intense love story. By doing so he managed to arouse interest in his social theories among readers who probably knew little about the Socialist philosophy—often labeled as Communism by a later generation—which he was convinced was undermining the foundations of American society. The fact that Dixon perceived these trends as early as the first decade of this century makes these novels of special interest to the student of cultural history.

In his books of non-fiction, in his novels, and in his public addresses, he consistently lamented the apathy of the American people toward Soviet-Marxist doctrines which, he said, might engulf the whole life of the nation. Even before the days of the Communist order, Dixon was distrustful of the explosive Russian political scene, for he stated in a sermon: "Politically, Russia is an unthinkable quality to the American mind. Her government is the contradiction of every principle for which our fathers fought and for which we live. She maintains with stubborn and fatal reactionery [*sic*] brutality, the most crushing and absolute tyranny outside of Turkey, Spain, and hell."[62]

During the 1930's, Dixon believed that Communists were infiltrating American government agencies. Though he had been a strong supporter of Franklin Delano Roosevelt and the National Recovery Act, he later maintained that the President was unknowingly surrounded by Communist influences. Seeing such a danger, Dixon answered an interviewer: " 'Communists control the Federal Theatre. . . . If you are an American and think as an American, you can't stay in it. The writers all bow to Lenin and Stalin and the Russian view of government.' "[63]

Dixon gave his final warning against the Communist evil in *The Flaming Sword* (1939). When Phil Stephens, the hero, sees America finally conquered by the "Soviet Republic of the United States," he realizes that the apathy of the citizenry has permitted this evil to creep into every facet of American life. As though Dixon were hurling one last warning to the United States, he closed the novel with Phil's words: " *'Communism is the collapse of the human mind under the pressure of modern life—a malignant, contagious mental disease now sweeping the world as the Black Death swept Europe in the Middle Ages.'* "[64]

In summary, Dixon's attacks on Socialism and Communism were not so clearly defined as his theories about the race problem were. He attempted to discredit Socialist theory by having it appear in a ridiculous or ludicrous light. In *The One Woman,* Mark Overman tries to show his Socialist friend Frank Gordon that Socialism undermines the roots of society. In the space of two pages, Overman quotes radical doctrines from Fourier, William Morris, Robert Owen, Grant Allen, and Karl Pearson. Dixon's theories on Socialism are revealed as Mark Overman selects from the writers passages which, the reader is to understand, are most objectionable to the author. Overman quotes from Fourier: " 'Monogamy and private property are the main characteristics of civilization. They are the breast-works behind which the army of the rich crouch and from which they sally to rob the poor.' "[65] Another quotation from Robert Owen reveals Dixon's main objections to Socialism: " 'In the new Moral World the irrational names of husband, wife, parent and child will be heard no more. Children will undoubtedly be the property of the whole community.'"[66]

Dixon maintained that Socialism undermines the foundations of the family. Without the family as the social unit, chaos will ultimately result. In pressing home the argument that Socialism weakens the basis of society, Overman tells Frank Gordon:

Observe in all these long-haired philosophers how closely the idea of private property is linked with the family. That is why the moment you attack private property in your pulpit your wife instinctively knows that you are attacking the basis of her life and home. Private property had its origin in the family. The family is the source of all monopolistic instincts, and your reign of moonshine brotherhood can never be brought to pass until you destroy monogamic marriage.[67]

Dixon also attacked Socialism as the undermining evil of the monogamous marriage in *The Way of a Man* (1919), in which Ellen West eventually finds sorrow and disillusionment where she had hoped to find ideal happiness through following a program of Socialist principles. The wife as the center of the home and the husband as its head is the most stable basis for an orderly society according to Dixon. Any departures from this arrangement can only bring a complete breakdown of moral and social values. The natural place for woman is in the home of a monogamic marriage, and those women who seek complete emancipation by following Socialist theory are "the sexless, the defectives, and the oversexed, who can always be depended upon to make the herd a lively place for its fighting male members."[68] If Dixon were living today, he would doubtless be writing effective satire about some of the more ludicrous aspects of the so-called women's liberation movement.

VI *Communism and Racial Conflict Combined*

The last of Dixon's published novels is in some aspects prophetic of the crises which have arisen with Russia since World War II and of current racial turmoil; for *The Flaming Sword* (1939) is a stark, hard-hitting account of Communist overthrow of the United States; and the Negro population is pictured as the main dupe of the Red menace. One of the announced purposes of the book is to trace the rise of Communism among the Negroes under the leadership of W. E. B. Dubois, whom Dixon describes as "a Red radical preaching dictatorship of the proletariat."[69] The title of the novel is taken from a sentence in Dubois' book, *Black Reconstruction in America,* which Dixon characterizes as "a blazing manifesto of Communism." Dixon said that *The Flaming Sword* was a sequel to *The Birth of a Nation* in which he continued the history of the conflict of color to the late 1930's. Dixon says in a prefatory note that he realized that he would be subject to attack: ". . . I have been compelled to use living men and women as important characters. If I have been unfair in treatment they have their remedy under the law of libel. I hold myself responsible."[70]

The interracial conflict is introduced early in the novel

when Dr. Cameron—the father of Ben Cameron, who was the hero of *The Clansman*—makes a speech denouncing the teaching of W. E. B. Dubois, the Negro educator. The racial problem is intensified as Angela Cameron Henry loses her baby son, her husband, and her younger sister through the violence of a Negro rapist, who is duly mutilated and lynched by a howling crowd of men. To regain some peace of mind, she secretly joins a Rosicrucian order in California. Her old friend, Phil Stevens, finds her at last and persuades her to come to New York. There her memory of the tragedy gradually fades as she becomes deeply interested in social work, and she tirelessly devotes her efforts toward improving the conditions of the slum sections of the city. Angela knows that Phil has always been in love with her; but, since the death of her husband, she feels that she can never love again. Phil aids her in her work and is always ready to help her promote some new scheme.

Through a young Jewess, Angela is introduced to a group of Communists and enters into the study of their principles. But, as she begins to see Communism from the inside, she becomes disillusioned and opposes the order as strenuously as she had defended it before. As Dixon develops the story, the Negro appears to Angela to be the easiest bait for Communistic doctrine. The Scottsboro trial is discussed, and the efforts of Communists to free the Negroes are described at some length. At the end of the novel, the Negro Communists under the name of the Nat Turner Legion take over the country by violence; and the Soviet Republic of the United States is in supreme authority.

For this novel Dixon had amassed a great array of news accounts from between 1900 and 1938, particularly those relating to racial conflicts. Actual race riots, rapings, and lynchings are interlarded with the plot. These accounts, continued until the time of publication of the novel, give the story a pressing sense of urgency and immediacy—an eleventh-hour quality that instills the credulous reader with fear. There can be little doubt that Dixon himself was sincerely apprehensive concerning what he interpreted as the disintegration of society through racial conflict. In a note to the advance "DeLuxe Edition," he implies that time is running out for a solution to the problem. Dixon seems, in this last published novel, to be making his last stand for the preservation of what he called "white civilization."

It is interesting to note that Dixon reveals in this novel he had been reading some of the current novels of the Realistic school which had caught the ear and the purse of the public. The raping and lynching scenes are described with shocking brutality that is beyond that of his earlier novels. Dixon is evidently attempting a new idiom with which to capture the attention of the "new reader." But this idiom does not seem to fit the author of widely popular novels of the preceding generation; for the mixture of raw Realism, not so evident in the earlier novels, with sentimentality for the "old South" weakens the effect of the work. When Dave Henry addresses his sweetheart as "Miss Angela," the reader is reminded of a type of fiction popular thirty-five years before in *The Leopard's Spots*. To a reading public now accustomed to the new Realism of the Naturalistic school, *The Flaming Sword* was an anachronism.

Although Dixon was highly ambitious for the novel, it failed to sell as well as his previous novels had. Few critics bothered to review the book at all; and, of those who did, most of them refused to take the novel seriously. One reviewer wrote that another novel by Thomas Dixon invited "news treatment rather than literary criticism,"[71] and another referred to it as a "nightmare melodrama" and "the expression of a panic fear."[72] In spite of several printings during the summer of 1939, *The Flaming Sword* sold poorly; and it remains as a symbol of the fickle moods and reading tastes of the public.

VII *Novels on "The New Woman"*

The right of women to vote and to have a larger share in determining the directions of society had become a lively issue in the nineteenth century; and the names of Elizabeth Cady Stanton, Lucretia Mott, Susan B. Anthony, Carrie Chapman Catt, and Lucy Stone are most prominent in the leadership of the movement. Although the struggle for the emancipation of women was particularly intense in

Great Britain and in the United States, these countries were not the first to grant women the right to vote. During the late nineteenth century and the early years of the twentieth century, four countries granted women the right to vote in national elections: New Zealand (1893), Australia (1902), Finland (1906), and Norway (1913).

By the second decade of the twentieth century, the "rights of women" had become a major political and social issue. Agitation of the question by suffragettes and retaliation by the opposition resulted in debates, arrests, and an attack on Buckingham Palace by Suffragettes in 1914. After more than half a century of women's suffrage in the United States, as guaranteed by the Nineteenth Amendment to the Constitution, it may be difficult for later generations to understand the intensity of the struggle for and against suffrage; but the extremities of the "Women's Liberation Movement" of this half of the twentieth century exemplify certain emotional facets of the struggle for suffrage. The ultimate reasons for the uncompromising stands for and against women's suffrage in the first two decades of this century may lie deep within the wells of Freudian psychology, and therefore beyond the purposes of this study; but, whatever the reasons, Thomas Dixon was found among the vociferous opposition. Dixon consistently wrote from the moralistic view that a woman is sullied when she participates in the materialistic maneuvering of a "man's world." The morality of womanhood, Dixon contends, is the last hope and protector of idealism; and woman would endanger civilization if she became degraded by descending to man's level. In his novels, he portrays woman, as we might anticipate, as a creature of finer clay than man and as "superior" to the baser instincts of the male; therefore, any attempt on woman's part to enter man's world only degrades her and makes her a slave to ambition.

Though Dixon wrote no trilogy of novels about "the new woman," he treats her in several of his works. In *The Foolish Virgin* (1915), a young woman, innocent of the ways of life, will not listen to the advice of her more sophisticated friend. Mary Adams, the innocent one, hotly retorts to her friend, Jane Anderson, that the books she reads are not cheap dime novels; some of her books had cost a dollar each! Her romantic, preconceived ideas about love and marriage lead her into an elopement with a charming criminal whose true nature she realizes as soon as they are married.

Dixon emphasizes very strongly in *The Foolish Virgin* the danger of an inexperienced woman's acting through uncontrolled impulses. Ready belief in the words of strangers is especially to be guarded against. Dixon weakens his thesis, however, by having Mary Adams accept the invitation of a "hermit" doctor to live with him for two years at his isolated lodge so that her child by her criminal husband, who has left her, may have a good start in life. This unusual relationship for some reason seems to present no problem either to Mary or to Dixon, and he makes no effort to justify or explain it.

The Fall of a Nation (1916), written during World War I, emphasizes the danger of following misguided idealists, especially if the idealists are women of pacifist instincts. Virginia Holland, a brilliant and beautiful young feminist, laughingly criticizes John Vassar, a congressman from New York, for his effort to introduce a bill in Congress for national defense. Miss Holland is the secretary for the "National Campaign Committee," a country-wide organization for the emancipation of women; and she wields great influence in her cause. Her compelling personality and power of public speech draw many people to her side as she campaigns against Vassar's plans for compulsory military training.

In this novel, Dixon sees a boundless gulf between the democratic and the monarchic state. He recounts the bitterness which the crowned heads of Europe feel toward America, and this bitterness finally reaches a climax as the monarchs of Europe join forces and invade the United States. The unsuspecting American people fall within a week to the mercy of the "Imperial Confederation." The feminine idealists who brought about America's downfall finally vindicate themselves, however, as secret word is passed over the country that on the anniversary of the *coup d'état* of the Imperial Federation each young American woman is to stab her unsuspecting foreign escort at the stroke of midnight. This spectacular and highly dramatic retrieval of power is unconvincing and allows the novel to end on a weak note.

The novel as a whole is, nevertheless, a fairly effective propaganda piece against unthinking pacifism and the troubles which attend indifference to political issues. The battle cry of the novel is "eternal vigilance is the price of liberty." The novel was widely read by the public, but the critics had little to say in its favor. One rather extreme criticism is at least indicative of the consensus of the reviewers: "It would be difficult to discover anything more futile and foolish than 'The Fall of a Nation,' even in the midst of an epoch that produces many futile and foolish books."[73] The book, which was also made into a motion picture (see Chapter 6), was instrumental in helping to crystallize the attitude of many people toward the war and toward the "emancipation" of women.

Another novel which may be included in the group dealing with womanhood is *The Love Complex* (1925), of which a reviewer said: "Erected upon the quicksand of untenable promises out of shaky conclusions continually tossed in the crosswinds of an untamed style, it cannot truthfully be described as an architectural masterpiece. As a study of love at first sight versus love that has 'ripened' it is probably one of the worst."[74] Such unfavorable criticism, however, did not greatly affect the book's popularity. It had a good sale, for, in spite of its obvious faults, it is not a story that can easily be laid aside before the end. The novel, "seasoned with a few dashes of pseudo-science and Freudianism,"[75] starts at a thoughtful pace which is maintained for about the first one hundred pages; but, from this point, the story plunges into depths of melodrama from which it cannot rise.

The narrative involves a young doctor, Alan Holt, who faces the supreme crisis of his life—should he devote himself completely and without ties to several years of medical experimentation, or should he marry Donna Sherwood? When he decides upon the first course, Donna agrees to wait for him; but, as time passes, she meets another young man with a fascinating personality. Before she realizes what is happening, she is drawn irresistibly to him, and they elope.

When Alan Holt learns of the elopement, he investigates the man's past and learns that he is a dangerous criminal. Alan pursues the pair to a lonely mountain hideaway; after Banning, the criminal, reveals his true nature, Donna is eager to return to Alan. This novel is quite similar in plot and situation to *The Foolish Virgin*, published ten years earlier.

The thesis of *The Love Complex* is that men are in many respects only slightly removed from their primordial state and that only through the greatest exercise of will may they escape the pitfalls of animalism. As a result, women have the responsibility of preserving men from such pitfalls. Donna Sherwood is a young woman drawn to her criminal lover only through physical attraction, without the concomitants of admiration and esteem. The book, though sometimes weak in structure, is one of Dixon's strongest novels about the pervasiveness of sex in human affairs and about the responsible role women have in "preserving civilization."

Dixon's most elaborate treatment of the "new woman" is found in *The Way of a Man* (1919). Ellen West is an unconventional woman who believes that a person should follow only one's personal code rather than the established moral one of society. She also believes in full equality and competition with men in every phase of business and social life. She contends that sex freedom is the supreme goal of the modern woman's movement. Ellen believes that the woman who is in earnest, the woman who is determined to gain the full rights of her sex, must demand freedom and independence. She boldly proclaims the theory of free love; and, when Ralph Manning asks her to marry him, she refuses him on the grounds that marriage is a degrading relationship of slavery for a woman and of authority for the man.

She readily accepts, however, a situation which has no ties or responsibilities attached. Manning will not agree at first to such a relationship, but she finally persuades him to see the matter her way; and they are "married" in a remote mountain retreat with the murmur of the brook beneath their cabin as their "wedding march" and the mist of the waterfall as Ellen's "bridal veil." Although the relationship continues several years, the constant secrecy and the deception which attend it cause the lovers to quarrel more and more. Finally, when Ellen's young niece comes to stay with her, Manning is attracted by the ingenuous, though conventional, attitude of the girl. Not until Ellen loses Manning does she realize how empty her ideals had been. Dixon treats the heroine sympathetically; in so doing, he is better able to show the disillusionment which finally comes to Ellen as she realizes the error of selfishly rebelling against the mores of society.

In spite of the attitudes which Dixon reveals in his novels about emancipated womanhood, he had earlier been so impressed by Carrie Chapman Catt, a woman suffragette against whom he had debated, that he saw the need for "inspired women leaders"[76] and decided to provide for the education of his sister Delia. He first sent her to study art at the Metropolitan Museum in New York, but her weak eyesight caused her to give up a career as an artist. He then sent her to an academy in New England, after which she attended medical college and became a pioneering female physician of national renown.

VIII   *Novels with Various Themes*

Dixon wrote several other novels treating social themes; but these, unlike the novels already discussed, do not fall into any thematic groups. *The Sins of the Father,* published in 1912, attempts to reveal the dangers of miscegenation; and this novel grew out of a successful play by Dixon produced two years earlier. In this story Major Norton has a daughter by Cleo, his mulatto housekeeper.

During the years that Cleo is in the household, Norton treats her with contempt because he blames her for having attracted him by her animal charm. Cleo's only real sin appears to have been that of a woman who loved "not wisely, but too well." With slight motivation, Dixon pictures Cleo's impulses as springing from evil instincts because she is of mixed blood.

Norton's wife had died years earlier; and his son Tom, now grown, meets and falls in love with Cleo's daughter and secretly marries her. Both father and son are so overwhelmed when it seems that a sister has married her brother that they believe that suicide is the only solution. Major Norton dies, but Tom survives to learn that his wife Helen is really not his sister—Cleo had secretly adopted another child after her own by Major Norton had died in infancy.

A departure from Dixon's novels of purpose is represented by *The Sun Virgin* (1929), a tale about the downfall of the great Incas in Peru. The historical background for the story appears to be drawn in large part from William H. Prescott's *The Conquest of Peru*. Through the historical tapestry is woven a sentimental tale of Yma, first among the Virgins of the Sun, and her love for Alonso de Molina, one of Francisco Pizarro's cavaliers. The author presents an interesting account of the manners and customs of the Incas and an array of historical facts.

The book becomes a panegyric for the glories of the Incas and a bitter indictment of the cruelty of the Spanish conquistadores at the execution of Atahualpa, the Inca ruler: "The Inca closed his eyes. The executioner circled his neck and strangled him to death while five hundred Spaniards pressed close murmuring their credos for the salvation of his soul."[77] To Dixon, the fall of the Incas was one of the most tragic developments in the establishment of European culture in the New World, and he closes the book with a depiction of desolation: "The storehouses are empty. Their roofs are gone. Their walls are broken, and wild beasts whelp and stable in their great bins. Couriers no longer speed from end to end of the empire. There are no roads. There are no resthouses. The vast flocks of pensive llamas that once grazed in the rich valleys have disappeared, slain in wanton folly. Where happy villages flourished with food, shelter, and clothes for millions, now stretches a desert steaming under the fierce heat of tropic skies."[78]

At his death, Dixon left an unpublished novel in which he bitterly attacked the Allied Powers for their treatment of the political problems in Turkey after World War I. "Facing East: A Story of a Great Adventure in Turkey" is a highly biased work showing Turkey as a noble nation beaten to her knees by the Allies and further degraded by the "atrocities" committed against her by the Greeks and Armenians. The book portrays David Lloyd George as an evil spirit intent upon the destruction of Turkish culture and nationalism; the young Turkish leader Kemal Ataturk is revealed as the apotheosis of courage and Turkish manhood; Admiral Bristol is highly praised for his sane handling of delicate diplomatic problems in Turkey arising from World War I.

Though the novel is a glorification of the Turks, the nominal hero is Hugh Preston, a free-lance American writer who has gone to Turkey to study the dangerous political situation arising from the occupation of the country by Allied forces. This occupation, Preston is told, was in violation of the treaty signed with Turkey at Mudros on October 18, 1918. Preston arrives in Turkey prejudiced against its people, but the intensely idealistic nationalism of Sirma Reisal, a beautiful red-haired Turkish girl, soon wins Preston to the Turkish side. The two young people fall in love, but Sirma feels that the great differences in their cultural backgrounds may bring them unhappiness. When a Greek army lands at Smyrna under the guns of the Inter-Allied fleet, Sirma tells Preston that she can never be a woman in love again until her people are free. Although Preston pleads with her, she is adamant; and she leaves him to join the Turkish revolutionary forces.

The Greeks are pictured as murderers and rapists as they occupy the country. The Turkish Nationalist movement under the guidance of Mustapha Kemal is treated at length, and the pitched battles between the Turks and the Allied forces occupy a large portion of the book. Sirma at last becomes reconciled to Preston and to the part taken by the American forces, as she sees the great suffering brought to thousands of Greek families who had lost their homes in the holocaust at Constantinople. After the marriage of Sirma and Preston, they have a child whom they name Kemal, after the "new father" of the Turkish people. The novel ends in a paean of praise to the man who had led Turkey out of the terrors of defeat to a new world of hope, ". . . the man of dazzling mind and constructive genius, the man of the century, a Turk, Mustapha Kemal."[79]

In "Facing East," Dixon reveals a knowledge of Turkish customs and ideals. His bias is obtrusive, however, and the unfavorable American attitude toward the Turks at the time the novel was written accounts for Dixon's failure to publish it: he was urged by friends not to publish because such action might well ruin his career as a writer. Dixon's sympathetic attitude toward Turkey under Kemal Attaturk contrasts with his highly critical attitude toward the regime of Abdul-Hamid II. In 1896, during the period of severe repression of the Armenians, Dixon had said: "The United States should move its ironclads on Turkey, and speak to the Sultan with lips of steel. We should take the Sultan by the throat and choke him into submission or kick him into oblivion."[80]

IX *Miscellaneous Works of Non-Fiction*

In addition to his novels and his religious works, Dixon wrote several other books. Though they are interesting as books per se, they add little to the understanding of the man's social philosophy or of his literary contributions. In 1932, in collaboration with Harry M. Daugherty, Dixon published *The Inside Story of the Harding Tragedy* in answer to a book written a short time before by Dixon's sister Mrs. Addie May Thacker. Gaston B. Means had told the story included in *The Strange Death of President Harding* to Mrs. Thacker; Means, whom Dixon called "the American Baron Von Munchausen," was implicated in the scandal concerning the theft of the famous Hope diamond and was at the time serving a sentence in the Federal Penitentiary in Atlanta. Dixon had urged his sister not to publish the book, which he believed had been built upon the fabrications of Means, and which reveals President Harding as the focal point of a vast amount of social and political scandal in Washington.

Dixon, who engaged in considerable research for his own book, studied over two thousand letters, documents, and affidavits. His purpose was to vindicate Harding, and he wrote in part: "It is one of the shameful pages in American history that a man who had loyally served his country, who had been honored by his fellow citizens and who had given them the best that was in him, should have been the object of such scurrilous and continuous slander."[81]

Dixon was also an admirer of Bernarr Macfadden, the

physical culturist; this admiration he expressed in his book *A Dreamer in Portugal* (1934). The work is an account of the experimental colony for fifty boys which Macfadden established at Estoril, Portugal, to demonstrate to the Portuguese government that she could regain her place among the great nations of the world by raising the physical and moral standards of her youth. According to Dixon's account, the experiment was a great success. To prove his point, he gives the menus for each day and at the end of the volume an appendix showing a comparative photograph and chart of each boy, based upon his mental and physical characteristics the day he entered the colony and the day he left three months later.

Dixon devotes a chapter to Macfadden's meeting with Mussolini in 1930, which is described as "one of the most remarkable scenes of the present generation."[82] Though Dixon's admiration for Mussolini later cooled, his respect for the dictator is here unreserved. Dixon considered the Italian leader a man of dynamic personality and tremendous physical vitality. The book is a panegyric on physical culture in general and on Macfadden in particular as the symbol of health and character. The work, which has the literary quality of a paid advertisement, is of no importance in the career of the writer.

Dixon glorified his great estate at Dixondale, Virginia, in *The Life Worth Living* (1914), a detailed account of his family life at Elmington Manor. He praises the virtues of country life as having a beneficent influence upon growing children. Numerous pets surrounded the family and servants, and the Dixons spent their leisure time in hunting, fishing, and horseback riding. Dixon describes his hunting exploits in detail; and he spends several chapters telling of the construction of several expensive sail and motor craft, especially of his yacht *Dixie* in which he took great pride. Although interesting in revealing Dixon's pastimes, the book is of little biographical value other than for revealing facts about a short period in his life.

The numerous works of Dixon and the versatility of his career attest to his wide range of interests in the issues of the day. Fortunately, most of the works lend themselves to classification so that his ideas may better be understood. Dixon's careers as minister, lecturer, and writer influenced millions of people and made his name a household word; but he was to make himself known to many more millions by his relationship to the theater and to the motion-picture industry.

CHAPTER 5

Playwright and Actor

I *"The Clansman"*

THE great success of *The Clansman* as a novel caused
Dixon to consider transforming it into a drama. After
studying the problem for several months, he characteristically
adopted a plan for producing a successful play. Enrolling
in a course in dramatic technique, he applied his energies
to the study of the principles of the theater. After several
weeks of intensive study and writing, Dixon submitted the
manuscript of the play to Crosby Gaige, who was at the time
on the staff of Alice Kauser, one of the best-known literary
agents in the country. Gaige, who was enthusiastic about the
possibilities of the play, submitted it to George Brennan, a
producer. A contract was drawn up in which Dixon received
half the stock of the Southern Amusement Company, the corporation which was to produce the play.[1] Before presenting
the play before the public, proof copies were sent to John Hay,
Secretary of State, and to Albert Bigelow Paine, the future
biographer of Mark Twain; and both men expressed their
admiration of the drama. The play followed very closely the
novel in its sensationalism, dramatic directness, and fast-
paced plot. The Romantic element, showing bravery and noble virtue triumphing over evil—largely Negroid—forces,
was calculated to appeal to the emotions of the mass mind.
The panoramic actions of the Klan in the novel offered what
at first seemed to be unsurmountable obstacles; but it was
hoped that a degree of verisimilitude could be achieved by
training four horses bearing Klansmen to gallop across the
stage on cue.

A certain success for the play was expected, but the opening night in Norfolk, Virginia, on September 22, 1915, was a tense experience for Dixon. Certain problems of the production had not been successfully solved by the opening date. One of the actors could not seem to learn his lines; and, the more he repeated them, the more confused he became. The four horses trained to gallop across the stage bearing members of the Ku Klux Klan seemed unusually nervous in surroundings strange to them, and the cast feared that, at any moment, the animals might leap over the footlights into the audience. Nevertheless, the first act concluded without mishap; and, as the curtain went down, the audience wildly cheered the play. When Dixon heard the applause at the end of the drama, he experienced one of the proudest moments of his life. As he said later, "What a tame thing [is] a book compared to this! There I saw, felt, heard, and touched the hands of my readers and their united heart beat lifted me to the heights."[2] He added that, though the novel might eventually reach five million readers, "the play if successful would reach ten millions and with an emotional power ten times as great as in cold type."

The Norfolk Virginian Pilot reviewed the play the next morning, September 23, 1905, under a seven-column heading across the top of the page: "THE CLANSMAN A TREMENDOUS SENSATION." Many people who had seen the play the night before attended the matinee performance. The receipts for the first week not only paid the entire cost of producing the play but also made a profit of fifty thousand dollars. Everywhere the play appeared, it created a sensation; and, as it moved through Charleston, Atlanta, Birmingham, and other Southern cities, people fought madly over seats; and policemen stood ready with fire hoses to drive back the crowds. Dixon was condemned on the one hand as "a servant of the devil"[3] and referred to on the other as the author of "the greatest theatrical triumph in the history of the South."[4]

When the play was shown in Montgomery, Alabama, on November 3, Governor Jelks of that state condemned the drama as a "nightmare."[5] A critic, writing in the *Montgomery Advertiser*, remarked caustically: "It is mere folly for

Tom Dixon to pretend that he is performing a public service in producing such a play. He is after dollars and he will get them. What a pity there is no way to suppress 'The Clansman.' "[6] The editor of the *Chattanooga* (Tennessee) *Daily Times* called the play "a riot breeder . . . designed to excite rage and race hatred."[7] On November 11, the editor of Knoxville, Tennessee, *Journal and Tribune* stated that "the only charitable conclusion" that could be reached concerning Dixon, who, he said, "never was well balanced," was that Dixon had "gone crazy."[8]

After a performance in New Orleans before a tumultuous crowd, with hundreds outside the theater unable to find seats, the play moved into the Middle West, where it played to overflow crowds. The simple fact was that, due to the enormous publicity preceding the play, no theater could be found large enough to accommodate the persons demanding to see the drama.

While the troupe continued through the West, Dixon returned to New York to help rehearse another cast for the New York opening scheduled for January, 1906. As a result of the unprecedented success of *The Clansman* in the South, Middle West, and West, the New York papers were filled with protests, pictures, editorials, and advertisements relating to the coming presentation. Despite the many objections offered by individual persons, *ad hoc* committees, and various organizations, the play opened on schedule on January 8 to the largest crowd ever to attend a performance at the Liberty Theatre. Unexpectedly, the New York theatergoers responded enthusiastically, filling the seats at every performance, night after night. The play was stopped in Philadelphia after a riot broke out in the theater.

Before the play was to open at the Wheiting Opera House in Syracuse, New York, Dixon had been warned by a friend that the company ran the risk of mob violence from the people of Syracuse. Before the Civil War, the Wheiting Opera House had been a famous station for the Underground Railroad by which Negro slaves escaped into Canada. As a result, opening night was tense; and every seat of the Opera House was filled well before the play began. Mob action, in which someone might be injured or killed, was feared by many members of the cast and of the audience; for the racial theme might at any moment provoke old enmities into angry violence. But the performance closed without incident, the people were enthusiastic, and the entire audience of the first floor insisted after the play on shaking hands with Dixon.

In 1906, when the drama was brought to Shelby, North Carolina, Dixon's home town, he accompanied the players so that he might learn the reactions of the audience. The response to the play was exuberant; only one person offered any criticism—Dixon's father. Gravely he spoke to Dixon: "My only criticism is, Son, I felt once or twice that you bore down a little too hard on the Negro. He wasn't to blame for the Reconstruction. Low vicious white men corrupted and misled him."9 When Dixon replied that he had tried to make the fact plain, his father replied: "I wish you had made it a little plainer. You couldn't make it too strong."10

It seems a paradox that *The Clansman* was as popular in the North as in the South, but the direct, emotional appeal to both the better and worse sides of man's nature was apparently overpowering. Perhaps, too, the popularity of the play is a significant commentary on the thought that Southern viewers had no monopoly on racial bias. The play so captured the minds of the theater-goers that for three years after the opening two companies toured the country simultaneously to sell-out crowds, creating a fortune for the author.

The commitments of Dixon, now a wealthy and famous man, drew him back to New York from his home at Dixondale, Virginia. Settling in a large brownstone home at 867 Riverside Drive, Dixon once more entered into the life of the great city. Never a person to be greatly concerned with his financial situation, he now thought that he had more money that he "could possibly spend."11 This idea, however, was soon dispelled. Dixon became interested in the New York stock market and invested nearly half a million dollars in several stocks, his heaviest investments being in United States Steel. While he was congratulating himself on having "a streak of commercial genius,"12 the stock crash of 1907 left him in serious financial trouble.

II *Other Plays*

Dixon now realized that he must take quick action if he were to save his home. He proposed to Brennan, the director of *The Clansman*, that they produce a play based on the novel *The Sins of the Father*, an idea which Brennan eagerly accepted; and Dixon began immediately rewriting the novel for stage presentation. When the play was first presented at Wilmington, North Carolina, in 1907, Dixon and the cast decided to remain a day or so to enjoy the surf at Wrightsville Beach. In the midst of their fun in the waves, the leading man of the play was killed by a shark; and Dixon, the only member of the cast who knew the dead man's lines, therefore took the leading part the next night at Fayetteville, North Carolina. The reviewers were so enthusiastic about Dixon as an actor that he decided to devote his time to acting. For nearly a year he toured with the company and acquired a great respect for the actor who often leads a lonely, monotonous life as he journeys with his company over the country to meet night after night every performance. The leading feminine role of the drama was played by a young woman who later married Dixon's son Tom.

On November 18, 1907, Dixon and Channing Pollock agreed to collaborate in writing a stage version of Dixon's novel *The Traitor*, the last novel in his trilogy about Reconstruction. Dixon was to receive forty-five per cent; and Alice Kauser, the agent, ten per cent. The names of the collaborators were to be printed on the drama in the same sized type, but Pollock's name was to be listed first. This play had a moderate success, but it failed to achieve the popularity of *The Clansman* and *The Sins of the Father*. Indeed, the drama which probably aroused the most comment of all of Dixon's plays after *The Clansman* was *The Red Dawn*, which was first presented at the Thirty-Ninth Street Theatre, August 9, 1919.

This play, based in part on Dixon's novel *Comrades*, begins on an island off the coast of California. John Duncan, a young political idealist, has founded a colony there to prove to the world that an ideal Socialist state can prosper. The drama opens quietly enough, for there is little to distinguish the colony from many Socialist colonies; but, when a delegate from the Central Soviet of Northern Europe arrives, trouble starts. Duncan precipitates an upheaval which threatens to destroy the colony. A quarrel arises among the leaders concerning the costumes to be worn by four dancing girls. The dance brings about a crisis, and Duncan's attempt to stop the dance is overruled. Stanton, an avid Leftist, takes command of the colony; and, when one of the dancing girls complains that Cargin, a lieutenant, has been executed without a trial, Stanton sends her to the stockade. Stanton now boldly asserts that the Socialists are going to overthrow the government of the United States and that Soviet troops are to march into Texas from Mexico to do so. When his wife tries to dissuade him from his purpose, Stanton has her imprisoned. A group of counter-revolutionaries overpower Stanton, while Simpson, a man who had joined the colony as an ex-convict, proves to be a United States secret agent and brings charges against Stanton. As the play ends, Simpson removes from his coat lapel the red bud of revolution and puts in its place the badge of a United States government official. The play, though at times weak in plot, is interesting as an example of Dixon's aversion before the end of the second decade of the twentieth century to Soviet principles. As in the novel *Comrades,* Dixon tries to make Socialist principles appear ridiculous or contemptible.

In *A Man of the People,* a play in three acts with a prologue and an epilogue, the prologue tells essentially the same story told in the prologue of *The Southerner,* Dixon's novel about Abraham Lincoln. The play effectively creates the atmosphere of pressure and confusion which surrounded Lincoln during his campaign for reelection. The first two acts take place in the President's room at the White House where Lincoln is beset by a constant stream of callers and petitioners. Captain Vaughan, who hates Lincoln and has aligned himself with the Copperhead faction, gains an audience with the President. Lincoln's character and personality so act upon the young captain that, instead of killing Lincoln as he had planned, he swears devotion to the President's cause.

The conflict between George B. McClellan and Lincoln constitutes a large part of Act II, in which Lincoln says that the presidential candidacy will be offered to McClellan if he will denounce the Copperhead group. Act III takes place in Jefferson Davis' headquarters in Richmond where Davis and Lee discuss the turn of the war, while Vaughan, now a secret agent for Lincoln, listens to their conversation. The news of Sherman's capture of Atlanta comes over the telegraph, and the Southern leaders realize that their cause is irrevocably lost. The epilogue of the play includes Lincoln's second inaugural address. The play ends as Lincoln concludes his historic message to the people. There is little in the play to distinguish it as dramatic art, with the exception of the interpretation of the character of Lincoln, which Dixon presents with considerable dignity and with appreciation for the burdens of the President.

In addition to his full-length dramas, Dixon wrote two one-act plays which should be mentioned: *The Almighty Dollar*, a short play on the evils of avarice, was copyrighted April 23, 1913; and *Old Black Joe*, the story of an old slave, was first presented in New York City, February 17, 1912.

Dixon's career as a playwright was mainly a by-product of his work as a novelist. His ability to dramatize his characters effectively is shown equally well in the novels and in the plays; but the weaknesses of his plots and the excesses of his sentiment are common to both forms of writing. The plays do not add anything new to the theses already set forth in the novels; for, in most cases, Dixon's adaptation of a novel for the stage was merely intended to present his message to a larger audience, for his avowed purpose as a writer was to reach as many people as possible.

In his ability as an actor, Dixon added to the stature of his career. Had he not terminated his experience behind the footlights so soon, he might have become more famous as an actor than he was as a novelist. Of a passionate, compelling, and dramatic nature, he dominated any scene in which he appeared. A newspaper reference praising Dixon's ability as an actor speaks for many persons who saw him perform: "Mr. Dixon had histrionic ability which indicated that his sphere in life was on the stage. His admirers believed he would have made a great actor. Eloquent in his presentation of any subject, with a commanding presence and power to move audiences, his friends were doubtless right in thinking his throne was the stage."[13]

But new horizons were constantly beckoning to this man of striking versatility, and he remained on the stage only long enough to satisfy himself that he could act. Disappointed in his youthful attempt to become an actor, he determined through the years to drive himself to eventual success. *Failure* was a word Dixon could not endure, and he would go to any lengths to avoid it. When he found that he had at last reached a goal he had long sought, he lost interest in the achievement. The life of an actor was exciting, but also it had its deadening, prosaic side. A play might reach a fairly wide audience, but the repetitions of plot and scene before relatively few people at a time made Dixon impatient of the drama as a medium for the dissemination of his ideas. Books were also too limited in their appeal. A new medium, motion pictures, was just becoming popular in the first decade of the twentieth century. What if this novelty could be given the dignity of a serious, historically vital story— would it not be a means of reaching far more people than could novels and plays?

CHAPTER *6*

The Birth of a Nation and
Other Motion Pictures

I *The Creation of a New Art Form*

DIXON spent two discouraging years searching for a producer for his motion-picture scenario based on *The Clansman*. Every established producer rejected it and wanted nothing of his "historical beeswax." The undeveloped taste of the public at the time was for low comedy and for one-reel farces, and the producers were hesitant to put money into ventures which they thought had no hope of success at the box office. As far back as 1911 Dixon had tried to form a corporation to be known as the Kinemacolor-Clansman Corporation for producing a film version of *The Clansman*, but Dixon could not arouse enough interest to get it established and operative.

After canvassing all of the well-known producers, Dixon started searching out the small, new, little-known companies. Finally, late in 1913, he met Harry E. Aitken who had just formed a small company but had not as yet produced any motion pictures. Aitken had hired a young man named D. W. Griffith, who had been filming one-reelers which he referred to as "sausages." Several years before Griffith had been hired and then dismissed as an actor in *The One Woman*. He was a Southerner from Kentucky and had been an enthusiastic reader of the novel. He therefore urged Aitken to let him see what could be done with Dixon's scenario. Dixon had been trying to sell the scenario for ten thousand dollars, but he reluctantly accepted a royalty contract because the company could not afford to pay him anything outright for the scenario. Dixon agreed to accept a twenty-five per cent interest in the picture as payment, a decision which eventually helped to make him a millionaire and paid him the largest sum ever received by any author for a motion picture.

After working for several weeks with Griffith in a dirty loft on Union Square in New York City which housed the Epoch Producing Corporation, the name of the little company, Dixon packed a trunk of papers and books of historical data for the film and gave them to Griffith. After the final arrangements had been settled in New York, Griffith left for Hollywood, California, where he planned to establish headquarters for making the film. From a studio on Sunset Boulevard, Griffith started recruiting actors, stagehands, and properties for the undertaking. The actors were as a rule inexperienced newcomers to motion pictures because Griffith could not afford experienced talents. When he had finally completed his recruitment, the following persons were selected to portray the main characters: Lillian Gish (Elsie Stoneman), Henry B. Walthall (Ben Cameron, the "little Colonel"), Mae Marsh (Flora Cameron, the "little sister"), Ralph Lewis (Austin Stoneman), Elmer Clifton (Phil Stoneman), Wallace Reed (Jeff the Blacksmith), Howard Gaye (General Lee), Raoul Walsh (John Wilkes Booth), Joseph Henaberry (Abraham Lincoln), and Donald Crisp (General Grant).

Griffith had hoped that the picture could be finished within a short time, but more than a year elapsed from the time he and Dixon had first worked on the scenario to the beginning of production. Because of the war in Europe, horses were difficult to obtain for the Ku Klux Klan scenes; and the thousands of yards of sheeting needed for the actors were extremely difficult to find. The greatest problem of all was the lack of money: three times production was suspended when funds were exhausted. Yet Griffith would not be deterred: "Besieged by mounting debts, hounded by creditors, discouraged by associates, he pushed the production to completion."[1]

In constructing the film story, Griffith took some ideas from *The Leopard's Spots*, included some reminiscences from his boyhood, and added them to the plot of *The Clansman*.

Working without any exact shooting script, he combined and condensed the material as he proceeded. Finally, after two years, the film was finished. The final actual shooting, however, had required only nine weeks between July and October, 1914. No actor had received more than seventy-five dollars a week.[2]

Griffith's directing revolutionized a hitherto static art. The motion picture prior to this film was comprised of a series of stilted poses taken at random distances and tagged together with little continuity, but Griffith introduced principles of shooting that made the motion picture an exciting new art form. Such technological devices as the "close-up," the "fade-out," and the "cut-back" are now accepted so readily that it is hard to imagine a period in motion-picture history when they did not exist; however, Griffith brought all of these devices to a level of high excellence in this picture. His camera, like a living eye, pried into the emotions of the characters and studied closely the features of the actor. The author of a definitive history of the film industry says of the picture: "It is life itself. From the beginning, shots are merged into a flux. Either the actions within the shots have some kind of movement or the duration of shots is so timed that the effect is one of continuous motion. This motion creates a 'beat' which accents the relationships of the separate elements of the film and produces a single powerful effect."[3]

When the film was finished, it was twelve reels long—an unheard-of length for that time. The expense of making the film prompted some critics to say that it was "a frightful waste and audacious monstrosity."[4] The picture under the title *The Clansman* was first privately shown at Clune's Auditorium in Los Angeles early in February, 1915. A few days later Dixon, Griffith, and about seventy-five guests were gathered in New York in a "huge, empty barn of a building" at Broadway and Fifty-third Street. Sitting in the cold, damp, semi-darkness of the theater, the guests were impatient to see the projectionist making ready his equipment. In one end of the large room, Joseph Carl Briel, the composer of the musical score for the picture, was wearily rehearsing the orchestra. Dixon had not seen any of the film, and he was apprehensive about its success. Not wanting to be unduly embarrassed if the film were a failure, he crept up into the balcony so that he could view the picture alone. But, when the last scene faded, the small audience was in an uproar; shouts of praise were called across the auditorium. Dixon, himself deeply moved, immediately caught the infectious enthusiasm of the group; he shouted to Griffith across the building that *The Clansman* was too tame a title for such a powerful story; it should be called *The Birth of a Nation*, the title which the motion picture subsequently bore.

II   *The Story*

The Birth of a Nation resembles *The Clansman* closely in spirit; but as already indicated, the plots diverge at some points. As a prologue, the film shows slaves being brought to America and the background of the Abolitionist movement leading up to the Civil War. When the main characters are introduced, Phil and Tod Stoneman from Pennsylvania are visiting the home of their school friends, the Cameron brothers, in Piedmont, South Carolina. Within a few scenes, Phil Stoneman falls in love with Margaret Cameron; and Ben Cameron becomes enamored of a daguerreotype of Phil's sister Elsie. Suddenly upon these idyllic scenes the horror of war erupts, and the Stoneman brothers hurriedly return home to join the Union forces. During the war, the two younger Cameron brothers and Tod Stoneman are killed. Matters now become ironically changed as we see Ben Cameron wounded and being nursed by Elsie Stoneman after he has been captured by Phil Stoneman. Phil's father, who in *The Clansman* was portrayed as Thaddeus Stevens, is in the film an evil figure who persuades the Negro Silas Lynch to lead an uprising against the Southern white population.

The looting and lawlessness during Reconstruction which Dixon had stressed in *The Clansman* are repeated in the film in vivid scenes of terror, greed, and brutality. Ben Cameron becomes the leader of the Ku Klux Klan; and, while trying to avenge some of the acts he has seen, he finds his sister Flora at the bottom of a cliff from which she has jumped in a desperate effort to escape Gus, a Negro servant. Silas

Lynch demands that Elsie Stoneman marry him when she comes to beg him to save her brother from the Negro militia who are holding him captive. The Klan, with Ben at its head, scatters the militia, frees Elsie, and lynches Gus. As the story closes, a double wedding takes place between the two families, symbolizing the joining of North and South into one Union.

In *The Birth of a Nation* the Negro is depicted as obnoxious and as but little removed from barbarism. The picture passionately maintains the principle of segregation as the only solution to the race problem. Biased as the film is, it is no wonder that it created such bitter controversy and was so widely seen and discussed. Cries of bigotry and intolerance followed Griffith and Dixon everywhere. On the other hand, there were many strong defenders of Griffith and Dixon and much praise for the authenticity of the film. A typical contemporary review says in part: "As an educator, its value is well-nigh inconceivable, and its chief value in this direction lies in its truthfulness. That the story as told by the picture is true I am ready to swear on the Bible, the Koran, the Zend, and all the other 'Holy Scriptures' put together. I know it is true, because I lived through the actual realities themselves."[5]

Another critic, writing more than twenty years after the film was first released, praised it highly and concluded: "The Birth of a Nation belongs to the nostalgic treasure house of American memories that will not be emptied into laps of the professors and documenters until the very last of a currently lively generation has been booted into the sunset."[6]

Oddly enough, both Griffith and Dixon stoutly maintained throughout the production and distribution of the film that their goal was to help heal the wounds of the nation by revealing the "misunderstood South" in its proper focus. The title which the film received is indicative of the optimism which Dixon and Griffith held for its sociological influence for good. In view of this optimism, Dixon and Griffith's reactions to the reception of the film are understandable. Griffith was so affected by the accusations that he had done a great disservice to race relations that he later spent nearly two million dollars producing *Intolerance*, a mammoth film of the incredible length of four hundred reels before cutting which tells, as the sub-title suggests, how "hatred and intolerance through the ages have battled against love and charity." Again, in *Hearts of the World*, a war picture produced in 1919, Griffith attempted to make amends for the bias of *The Birth of a Nation* by having a white soldier kiss a dying Negro boy. But the damage, intentional or not, had been done; and the reputation that *The Birth of a Nation* acquired as a goad to racial tensions makes it a controversial motion picture to this day.

III   *Troubles with Censorship*

Before the film could be scheduled for its first public showing, news of its artistry and explosive content began to spread rapidly. Oswald Garrison Villard, editor of the New York *Evening Post*, and Moorfield Storey, president of the American Bar Association, led the attack to prevent the release of the film because they thought it would incite riots. The management of the Epoch Producing Corporation met to discuss means of getting around the growing opposition. Within a few days of the scheduled opening, it looked as though the "sectional conspiracy,"[7] as Dixon called it, would be successful in suppressing the film.

In the middle of the crisis, Dixon thought of his friend Woodrow Wilson, now President of the United States. If Wilson could be persuaded to see and approve the film, perhaps the opposition could be overcome. Dixon wrote Wilson requesting a thirty-minute interview; and, when he received Wilson's permission a few days later, Dixon journeyed to Washington to lay the matter before the President. Wilson was somewhat puzzled to learn that Dixon wanted him to view a "movie," but he said he would be glad to do so as a personal favor. He referred to the day when, years before, Dixon had recommended to the Board of Trustees at Wake Forest College that Wilson be awarded an honorary degree; for the publicity, as has been noted, came at a crucial time in Wilson's career and helped place him in national prominence. Wilson said that he would not be able to go to a public viewing of the film because his wife had recently died; but, if the projection equipment could be brought to the East Room of the White House, he would view the film there. The motion picture was shown on February 18, 1915, to Wilson, his daughter Margaret, and to the members of the President's cabinet and their families. When the film showing was over, Wilson said: "It is like writing history with lightning. And my only regret is that it is all so terribly true."[8]

The fact that the President had viewed the film would be a powerful deterrent to the persons who were seeking to stop the public showing, but Dixon wanted to get as much help as possible. He arranged through Josephus Daniels, then Secretary of the Navy, to obtain an interview with Douglas White, Chief Justice of the Supreme Court, who had a reputation as a gruff man who had little patience with trivialities. When Dixon announced that he wanted Justice White and the other members of the Supreme Court to view a motion picture, White interrupted him: "Moving picture! It's absurd, Sir. I never saw one in my life and I haven't the slightest curiosity to see one. I'm very busy. I'll have to ask you to excuse me."[9] Dixon was about to leave White's office when he remarked that the film was about the original Ku Klux Klan. At these words, White pushed his work aside and said slowly that he had been a member himself; he then said he wanted to see the picture. That night the film was shown in the Raleigh Hotel to the members of the Supreme Court and of the Senate and the House of Representatives.

The audacious moves of Dixon in having the President, the Supreme Court, the Senate and the House of Representatives see the film served him well in the weeks that followed. Forty-eight hours before the film was to have its first public showing, Dixon learned that the theater would be closed on opening night. When a defense attorney for the Epoch Producing Corporation remarked that *The Birth of a Nation* had already been shown at the White House, the opposition was incredulous. When the fact was corroborated by a telephone call, Chief Police Magistrate McAdoo ordered the police to protect the premiere against interference.

The world premiere of *The Birth of a Nation* opened at

the Liberty Theater in New York on March 3, 1915; and the movie immediately became the sensation of the hour. The response was overwhelming; for, as one critic wrote, "People had not realized that they *could* be so moved by what, after all, is only a succession of photographs passed across a screen."[10] Discriminating viewers saw that film was a new art form more powerful and pervasive than any other medium in the history of mankind. They also saw the great potential in this new medium which had become so powerful so fast.

The controversy which raged over the theme of *Birth of a Nation* (that the Negro was inherently inferior and should be kept in a subservient state) made the nation aware of the tremendous social import of the film. As great as the controversy was, it was overshadowed by the universal acclaim for the artistry of the picture. On every hand critics praised its pulsating, structural unity. The techniques introduced or brought to a high stage of development in the film became the touchstones for all motion pictures in the years that followed.

Soon after the release of the picture, race riots and trouble with the censorship boards in various cities began. When the film was first shown in 1915 at the Tremont Hotel in Boston, a riot occurred during which the police fought with a crowd of ten thousand people for twenty-four hours. The publicity arising from this incident boosted the notoriety of the film tremendously. Tension ran high wherever the film appeared, and Griffith and Dixon were loudly denounced. In many cases where the problem of censoring the film arose, the boards announced that the nature of the picture was not under their jurisdiction. W. D. McGuire, Executive Secretary of the New York Board of Censorship, made public the following statement after the Board had finally passed the film: "A Board of Censorship for motion pictures or dramatic productions should confine itself entirely to the consideration of whether a given production is objectionable from the standpoint of public morals. If it can pass this test, it should be permitted. If not, it should be stopped. Public authorities have no more right to interfere with the production of a play or a motion picture which emphasizes the southern point of view of our great conflict and the subsequent period of reconstruction, than that of a play which lays emphasis upon the northern part of view."[11]

Moorfield Storey, President of the American Bar Association, led a determined fight to suppress the picture in Massachusetts. He summoned a crowd of twenty-five thousand people before the state capitol and demanded that Governor David Walsh act against the film. The governor immediately laid the matter before the Massachusetts State Legislature and asked for a law to prevent the showing of the film. The matter was pressed through the legislative body, but the Judiciary Committee of the state found the bill unconstitutional.

Everywhere throughout the West the picture met opposition, but in the months following the premiere showing in New York, no theater was permanently closed to *The Birth of a Nation*. At first refused in Chicago, the picture was shown under a permanent injunction restraining police interference if children under eighteen were not admitted. It was also forbidden for a time in St. Louis, and a city official spoke of the lengths to which he went in order to keep the film out of the city: "It took three municipal departments, the Police Department, the Recreation Division, the Prosecuting Attorney's office, all the reviews on the film which I had at hand or could obtain by telegraphing for, and a good many consultations and conciliations to keep it out."[12] The company spent thousands of dollars in legal fees, but it gained rewards many times greater. Twelve companies had to be organized to handle the assignments for the film at motion-picture houses throughout the country.

The Birth of a Nation was the first film to charge a two-dollar admission fee at a time when the average cost of admission was about fifteen cents. The incredible popularity of the film made stars of the actors, millionaires of the producers, and may have earned more money than any other film in motion picture history.[13]

IV *The Motion-Picture Producer*

Before long, differences of opinion between Griffith and Dixon led to strained relations; and Dixon decided to go his own way and to out-do his co-worker in making motion pictures. Griffith's great success with *The Birth of a Nation* had changed him considerably and had made him a difficult man with whom to deal, as one critic has noted: "That spirit of inquiry and humility which once had been his outstanding trait was replaced by a spirit of self-aggrandizement and ostentation. He began to concentrate upon exploiting his personality and reputation; it made no difference what he did, as long as the name 'Griffith' appeared in print."[14] Dixon moved in 1917 to California and built "The Dixon Studios, Laboratory and Press," an impressive array of buildings, at Sunset Boulevard and Western Avenue in Los Angeles, where he planned a motion picture to outrank *The Birth of a Nation*.

As discussed in Chapter 4, Dixon published in 1916 *The Fall of a Nation*. He adapted the novel for the screen so that he could warn a larger segment of the public concerning the danger of taking a pacifist approach to World War I. The film proved to be very popular, though in no sense did it receive as much attention as had *The Birth of a Nation*. As Dixon said of the new film, "It reached more than thirty-million people and was, therefore, thirty times more effective than any book I might have written."[15] Apparently Dixon was equating popularity with influence, but the picture must be counted a failure by the standards Dixon had set to make it excel *The Birth of a Nation*. And, when Dixon produced in 1918 a film version of his novel *The One Woman*, published fifteen years earlier, the film did not arouse as much controversy as the novel had because the propriety of the subject (the "new woman" espousing "emancipation" and "free love") was not so questionable as it had been earlier; but it is interesting in that Dixon employed some new techniques in photography such as a process for speeding up the development of the film and the extended close-up study of the faces of the actors.

During the next several years, Dixon produced two other motion pictures. Adapting the criticism of Socialist principles from his novel *Comrades*, published in 1909, he met the growing postwar Bolshevist influence by producing a motion picture in 1919 based on the book. The original title was *Bolshevism on Trial*, but the film was released as *Comrades*.

On June 1, 1923, when Dixon addressed the Author's League of America at Town Hall in New York City, he declared that motion-picture stories were ten years behind the technological developments of the industry. In *The Mark of the Beast*,[16] Dixon said that he had tried to put those technological advances to the best use. In this film he sought to preserve better unity of action and character by using only five actors. The thesis that man's nature is dualistic, one good, the other bad, is set forth in the story. The young doctor in the tale believes that "while man sleeps the beast awakes." This "beast" in man affects the lives of the characters in New York City and the Catskill Mountains.

The Mark of the Beast is especially interesting in that Dixon made a "psychological" study of his characters, a method of approach which has become common among motion-picture producers in recent years. Dixon had also attempted to heighten his effects by utilizing the changes in lighting techniques recently made available to the industry. Though he had optimistically tried to bring the motion picture "up to date," he had overestimated the ability of his audience to understand his methods. At the premiere showing of the film in June, 1923, the young heroine, years later to become Dixon's second wife, accurately predicted the motion picture's reception by saying that the film was too advanced psychologically for its time and that it would fail at the box office.

One of Dixon's scenarios which did not reach the screen deserves notice because it appears to have been well suited for presentation. "The Torch"[17] is a rather detailed account of John Brown's campaign and his subsequent seizure of Harper's Ferry. In the story Brown appears as a fanatic who makes the most of his martyrdom before his execution at Charlestown, Virginia. Dixon places most of the blame on Brown for having touched off the "powder keg" that caused the Civil War. "The Torch," "written directly for the screen," might have made a popular motion picture, for later treatments of John Brown's career in literature and on the screen attest to the public's interest in the man.

Dixon's desire to surpass *The Birth of a Nation* was never fulfilled. Nor did D. W. Griffith ever again reach the success which was his when he collaborated with the author of *The Clansman*. The peculiar genius of each man was transmuted through their collaboration into an artistic performance of greatness that neither of them afterward achieved separately. Dixon remains as an important, though transitional, figure in the history of the film industry. To understand the meteoric growth of the popularity and cultural impact of motion pictures during the second and third decades of this century, some attention must be given to Dixon's influence. His career in motion-picture work occupied only about a decade of a long life filled with many endeavors, and this fact reminds us again of the amazing versatility of the man.

V   *The Influence of Motion Pictures*

The tremendous success of *The Birth of a Nation* had convinced Dixon that motion pictures were the most powerful medium ever devised for education. With the dissemination of ideas of truth and idealism throughout the world, man would understand his neighbor better and wars would become fewer. The terrible holocaust of World War I and the constant turmoil in the nations of the world alarmed Dixon and made him fear for the future of mankind. Hate, greed, and misunderstanding, said Dixon, would destroy the world if something were not done to prevent future wars. He looked with foreboding toward a second world war which, he thought, must inevitably come; his words, written in 1935, have something prophetic about them:

In the next war the destruction of the civilized population behind the front will be the first object of the attacking army. This destruction will be effective and horrible beyond all powers of the imagination to conceive it.

The science of war will then reach its logical climax. It will kill by wholesale, not retail—thousands in an hour. It will kill without mercy. Mercy is a sentiment—war is a science.

When we realize the fundamental unity of the world, we know that if civilization does not end war—war may bring an end of civilization.[18]

The only way for civilization to end war, Dixon thought, is to educate the masses of the world in all nations. But, since education is a slow, uncertain process, the world might well be destroyed before man could achieve universal understanding. The answer as to how an educative process could be instituted by which man could be quickly taught the meaning of the history of mankind and as to how he might be shown the evils that beset civilization lay, Dixon said, in the motion pictures, which could appeal to ". . . the dark skinned hordes of Abyssinia, the yellow millions of the Far East, the dreamers of India, the warriors of Islam, the hosts of Russia, Europe and the two Americas"[19]: "We can make them see things happen before their eyes until they cry in anguish. We can teach them the true living history of the race. Its scenes will be vivid realities, not cold words on printed pages, but scenes wet with tears and winged with hope."[20]

In motion pictures, man had at last a universal language; and, to institute this great education program, no ponderous legislative action would be needed, no expenditure of great sums of money for the erection of buildings for the new "University of Man." "The class rooms, with row on row of seats in our Theatres, are already heated and lighted and provided with ushers."[21]

Unfortunately, Dixon was not to see his ideal educational system realized. He frequently deplored the degrading influence in the motion picture and in the theaters, and he spent considerable energy trying to improve the moral and ethical qualities of the drama. Dixon's insight into the pervasive power of motion pictures is vindicated in the saturation of our present culture by television. What Dixon did not visualize is the incredible power of "pictures on a screen" brought daily into millions of homes, hour after hour, day after day, to wield an influence beyond anything even Dixon dreamed. Dixon saw motion pictures as the most powerful medium of communication ever devised, and he may have been right in saying that civilization could be transformed by the wisest use of this medium; but he also realized that no instrument can rise above its purveyors. If Dixon were living today, he would doubtless decry the emphasis in television news coverage upon what is vicious and sensational.

To all the questions about how to improve the moral quali-

ty of the novel, the drama, and the motion picture, Dixon
had no ready answer. As he grew older, he saw increasingly
the need for effectively curbing the pernicious influence
of some forces; but censorship was not the answer. Only
by man's becoming aware of his great moral responsibilities
to society, Dixon thought, could he effect any permanent
change for good. That Dixon was himself often accused of
inciting the primal passions of men is another paradox in
this man of contradictory and complex personality. Ironically, some of Dixon's works came to be regarded as representative of the very evils which he strenuously denounced;
for a critic has said of his fiction: "His realism is the realism of the open sore; his art the art of the billboard."[22]

CHAPTER 7

The Last Years

I "Wildacres"

DIXON'S motion-picture venture had not achieved the success for which he had hoped, so, having maintained his home at 867 Riverside Drive in New York while producing films in Hollywood, Dixon moved the center of his operations to New York in 1920. The proceeds from his novels, plays, and the film *The Birth of a Nation* had made him a very wealthy man. But he did not remain wealthy; for, despite talent for making money through the years, he was not careful about retaining what he had made. Generous and expansive in spending money, he sometimes found himself short of the funds he needed; yet, when his money was depleted, he could call upon his creative brain for a new money-making project. He gave large sums to charitable and civic organizations, invested heavily for a time in stocks and bonds, and provided generously for his family. Jordan, Dixon's younger son, had been crippled by poliomyelitis since early childhood; and Dixon, who sought every means to cure him, spent large sums of money for doctors and for treatments to restore health to his son; but his expenditures were useless. Jordan, a handsome, appealing young man, died March 18, 1919.

Early in 1925, Dixon, who had read of the great real-estate development of Coral Gables, became enthusiastic about the land boom in Florida. He invested heavily in a land company, though he had only a hazy knowledge of the location of his property. Before he was able to pursue his interests in the new venture, the death of his brother Frank on

May 23 caused him to lose all enthusiasm for the project. Only three weeks after Frank's death, Dixon's older brother Clarence died also. The death of both brothers in so short a time incapacitated Dixon; and, dejected in spirit, he journeyed to western North Carolina in the hope that the restful mountain scenes would dull the edge of his grief. Settling temporarily in Asheville, he roamed the hills day after day in a kind of thoughtless abstraction.

As the sharpness of his grief lessened, he became interested in the possibilities of the region as a site for a great colony of writers, artists, and creative thinkers. The Little Switzerland district, in the shadow of famous Mount Mitchell, seemed ideal for such an establishment. The interest in tourism was beginning to sweep the country, and Dixon became enthusiastic about the project. He purchased a large tract of land on the ridge opposite Mount Mitchell, named it "Wildacres," and soon began to invest large sums of money in developing the site. The area, about seven miles long, contained "three mountain ridges, two valleys, six peaks, and three streams of crystal water."[1] The ravines, hills, and valleys were covered with a variety of wild flowers and trees.

In this beautiful setting Dixon planned to establish a forum for the free discussion of art, science, philosophy, religion, and politics. In outlining his plan for the great project, Dixon explained his goal: "Its ideal will be the renewal of Life through the inspiration of Nature. Its discussions will not be over the heads of the people. They will not be bound by the fetters of the narrow mind. Nor will they be allowed to degenerate into loose thinking. Around the auditorium and along the slopes of the beautiful mountain on which it will stand and across the brooks that ripple through the dense woods at its foot, the Association will build log and rustic cottages for authors, artists, scientists, educators, and students."[2] Dixon planned to build a large hotel, to construct an elaborate system of waterworks, electric lights, and sewerage; he hoped to install swimming pools, tennis courts, stables, garages, and golf courses. In his initial report to the public about the project, he announced that three hundred lots had been surveyed on Pompey's Knob, Rhododendron Drive, Azalea Avenue, and Laurel Road, and that these lots were ready for immediate building.

"Wildacres" was to be a kind of permanent Chautauqua establishment which would attract thousands of people who would come to enjoy the scenery, sports, and intellectual stimulation provided by outstanding speakers and teachers. Because of the great size of the establishment, a number of famous people could be expected to be in attendance at all times, thus guaranteeing a large attendance by the public. Discussion groups in writing, science, art, and history were only a few of the many intellectual attractions which "Wildacres" was to provide. Dixon described the project in enthusiastic terms and wrote letters to scores of prominent persons, enlisting their influence and support; and he energetically campaigned for the program throughout the state. As a result, the members of the association which he formed included some of the leading educators and public figures of the day.

The project began to take impressive form: several large buildings were erected; elaborate facilities were installed. Dixon had invested much of his wealth in the program when the end of the land boom abruptly came. People who had been eagerly buying property suddenly lost interest; Dixon's land in Florida became worthless; and the stock market fluctuated erratically. The project that might have made Dixon a multimillionaire was, almost overnight, a millstone about his neck; and there was little to salvage from the venture. Stunned, bewildered, and faced by the realization that his wealth was gone, he returned to New York, wondering what he could do next. Now past middle age, he saw that he must begin once more to rebuild his fortunes.

II *Politics Once More*

Added to the oppression of his financial troubles was an even more poignant one: his wife Harriet suffered an illness which was to make her an invalid for the rest of her life. The death of his son Jordan, then of his brothers Frank and Clarence, had depressed Dixon greatly; but the illness of Harriet made his resolution for achievement much more difficult to generate. The tenderness that he bore his wife is expressed in the dedication of one of his books: "Dedicated to my wife, in whose dear person the day-dreams and ideals of my boyhood live as the sweetest reali-ties of manhood, the inspiration of whose love, as the voice of God, called me from the valley of the world's ambitions to the heights of nobler aims, unto her, with tenderest love, this book I bring, a sheaf from the first fruits of that better life."[3]

In Dixon's renewed determination to regain his wealth, he applied himself tirelessly to writing additional books; but they were no longer the best-sellers that the others had been in the first two decades of the century. The nov-elist was now producing outdated works in the afterglow of his fame. The issues that had been so vital to the nation through World War I now faded before the Depression of the early 1930's, and the school of Southern chivalry and romance to which Dixon had belonged no longer attracted so many readers as in the past.

Seeing that he must make his living by other means, Dixon, after a period of non-participation for nearly half a century, once more became an active participant in politics. In 1932 he campaigned for Franklin D. Roosevelt, the man who, Dixon said, could lift the country out of its depression, both financial and mental. The Roosevelt family influence was not new to Dixon, for it will be recalled that while still a young minister in New York, he had become a friend of Theodore Roosevelt. The men had formed a rather close attachment, and when Theodore Roosevelt ran for the gov-ernorship of New York, the vice-presidency of the United States, and finally the presidency, Dixon was a strong sup-porter. So long as his father lived, Dixon never told him that he had voted for a Republican because to the elder Dix-on the word "Republican" continued to be synonymous with "Reconstruction." Dixon greatly admired Theodore Roose-velt; and, when another Roosevelt, a Democrat, was elected to the presidency, Dixon said that he felt as though the millen-ium had arrived at last. Franklin D. Roosevelt's energetic re-organization of the government caused Dixon to say that the President was staging a bloodless revolution, that the country would be able to rise above the Depression under his peerless leadership.

So enthusiastic did Dixon become about Roosevelt's program that he made a nationwide speaking tour in 1934 as a special representative of the National Recovery Administration. Now seventy years of age, he was still handsome and impressive in appearance. For the remainder of his active life, his erect, commanding figure and his abundance of white hair made him the cynosure of every crowd. His absence from the lecture platform had not dulled his eloquent delivery; he spoke in terms of ringing conviction about the hopes and the achievements of the National Recovery Administration.

The conviction had grown upon Dixon by 1936 that the government was becoming infiltrated with Communist and other destructive elements. In addition, the governmental agencies, Dixon thought, had so grown in complexity and bureaucracy that it was impossible for Franklin D. Roosevelt to understand what was happening. Dixon therefore withdrew his allegiance to the Democratic party and agreed to represent the first district of North Carolina at the National Republican Convention in Cleveland, Ohio, at the request of the Republican chairman. On October 12, 1936, in a speech at the Wake County, North Carolina, courthouse, Dixon spoke on behalf of the Republican Party, "which by his own confession, he [had] fought to destroy for fifty years."[4] Dixon said that he was glad that the Republican party had not been destroyed " 'because that is the only instrument that can be used to destroy the New Deal. I think this New Deal is all wrong. I am full of fire and pizen.' "[5]

In the 1936 Presidential election, Dixon campaigned for Alfred M. Landon. Dixon said that he had always considered himself a Democrat but that the New Deal administration had finally forced him to desire another leader. As a result of his support of the Republican candidate, Dixon the following year received from Judge I. M. Meekins, a Republican, an appointment as the clerk of the United States District Court in Raleigh. On May 1, 1937, after leaving his New York home, Dixon assumed his duties in Raleigh where exactly fifty years before he had preached his first sermon in the Second Baptist Church. In his new position, Dixon succeeded Captain S. A. Ashe, a ninety-seven-year-old Democrat who had resigned after nineteen years of service. Dixon, now seventy-three years of age, still looked forward to a long period of literary activity. Upon accepting the position, he said: " 'The position will be a backlog of security for a long range plan of writing—a sort of 20-year program all my own.' "[6] He had stated earlier that he was spending old age " 'in an endless passion for work—for new thought and new ideas and new achievement.' "[7] The fire of his earlier years still remained with him, and he moved with the agility of a young man. His sparkling eye and distinguished bearing soon made him a familiar figure in the city. He hoped that his new experience would provide him with the leisure and background of human interest and history from which he could draw his stories.

III   Illness and Death

On December 29, 1937, Dixon's wife Harriet died after a long illness. A little more than a year later, on February 26, 1939, Dixon was stricken by a cerebral hemorrhage in his suite in the Sir Walter Hotel. His condition remained so critical that the doctors advised that he not be moved. For weeks he lay in the hotel, unable to raise himself from the bed. Miss Madelyn Donovan, who years before had played the feminine lead in Dixon's motion picture *The Mark of the Beast,* had been for the past year a deputy clerk in the Federal Court in Raleigh and a research assistant for Dixon's forthcoming novel, *The Flaming Sword.* Seeing him now in a helpless state and realizing that his need of aid would be great in the future, she married him at his bedside on March 20, 1939. Partly recovering from his attack, Dixon attempted to direct his clerkship; but in 1943, in his seventy-ninth year, he finally had to relinquish his work entirely. The remaining years of his life were ones of physical suffering and of mental torture because he could not be active as in the past. His wife assumed his duties as clerk and spent her energies in trying to make him comfortable.

The days of recognition were now past, for Dixon had outlived 'his fame. He had seen social issues and literary tastes come and go; his novels, which had once aroused so much controversy, now gathered dust on the library shelves of the nation; and royalties no longer arrived. He had hoped to reestablish himself in his old age by publishing *The Flaming Sword,* but he was too ill to seek a good publisher who might place the book in advantageous outlets. The autobiography, upon which he spent many hours reminiscing of his past active life, lay unrevised. The wealth which had bought him fine homes at 867 Riverside Drive in New York and at Dixondale, Virginia, was now gone. In his trunks lay stacks of bonds that once had paid large dividends but were now worthless.

But Dixon did not lament the loss of wealth; money had never been of great importance to him. The sense of ownership was lacking in his make-up, for he never bought houses or furniture as though they were to belong to him. With reference to wealth, Dixon had said: "In my relation to material property there has always been a screw loose in my make-up. I've always been able to make money but never tried to hold it. When times got hard I've always been able to say to myself: 'Cheer up, old boy, you'll soon be dead. And what of it?' If I should die tomorrow with my last breath I'd say: 'My love to the world.' I have lived a thrilling adventure called life. The cycle ends. A new one begins. For I shall live again."[8] Only in the happy hours when he had sailed his boats at Cape Charles did the awareness of possession take hold; with boats he felt a "oneness," a sense of identity that he found nowhere else.

As the days went by, Dixon became weaker and took less interest in his surroundings. For long periods he subsisted on nothing more than egg white stirred into orange juice, but he occasionally rallied and asked for solid food. In his eighty-second year, on April 3, 1946, Dixon ceased the long struggle for life.

CHAPTER *8*

A Summing-Up

I *Dixon's Complex Personality*

IN seeking out the matrix from which Thomas Dixon was formed, to assess him as an extraordinary instance of human nature, we run the risk of acceding to the popular demand of the current period for historical psychoanalysis, particularly of the Freudian school. To place the Olympian finger upon the nerve of the human psyche of a living person and say *"This* makes him tick" is fraught with risky permutations, but to do so with persons long dead may be presumptive—if not altogether preposterous. Nevertheless, there are doubtless many critics who could quickly read Dixon and who could immediately pigeonhole him. They would refer to him as a product of his early environment, citing the sternness of his father as an Oedipal explanation of Dixon's own attitudes, particularly in sublimating his frustrations in racial prejudice. This form of psychoanalysis would find ready acceptance among many readers, as the popularity of many current, sensational biographies attests. Such explanations are readily accepted because, like the older Hollywood film script, they make everything seem to work out neatly at the end.

But there is a flaw: though the other Dixon children necessarily shared the same environment and family relationships that Thomas did, his brothers did not share a number of his attitudes. For example, Clarence Dixon showed little of the bias toward Negroes which is such a strong feature in Dixon's novels. When a Negro woman applied for membership in his Brooklyn Church in 1902, Clarence Dixon stood staunchly with the one other person who favored her admission. About another occasion which caused a furor at the time in the South, Clarence Dixon commented: "When President [Theodore] Roosevelt invited Booker T. Washington to dine with him, he did an act for which I admire him. I admire him for his courage."[1] Thomas Dixon, on the other hand, wrote a vigorous letter to his friend President Woodrow Wilson objecting to Wilson's hiring of Negro employees in the Treasury Department.[2]

Dixon has also been called "a child of Reconstruction," and his attitudes in maturity are said to be direct byproducts of the "stern truths" he had learned during that period. Such a view has something to recommend it, for Dixon reached his most impressionable age during the Reconstruction era; and the events of his young boyhood remained with him so vividly that they became a basis for his career as a novelist. But we must be careful not to say that here lies the final secret of Thomas Dixon, for many other persons who were at their "most impressionable age" during Reconstruction came away with a different orientation. The tenuous threads which weave the uniqueness of human personality are referred to by Dixon as he wrote of an acqaintance who, as a boy of fourteen, "ran away from home to enter the Civil War. He fought twenty-six pitched battles through four years of strife and came out at eighteen, a veteran soldier but still a laughing boy. . . ."[3] Dixon, who was fascinated by the intangibles which make one person different from another, began, in writing his memoirs, to try to account for his own uniqueness. He wrote that his pulse was so abnormally slow from his earliest years that he always had difficulty in getting physicians to approve him for life and medical insurance. Ironically, he attributed his boundless energy for work and his long life to this slow pulse rate.

The indomitable vein of iron in the personality of Dixon was such that he antagonized many people by his uncompromising will, but his firmness also made him highly respected as a man of principle. A relative said that "a personality as strong as his was most conflicting at times and the turmoil within him intense. . . . [He] was a man who never knew what failure was even though he experienced it many times."[4] He was, as he admitted, "a reactionary individualist," sometimes "full of fire and pizen"; but those who knew him intimately spoke of his generosity, his irresistible charm, and his tenderness. We may be closest to the truth in saying that Thomas Dixon seems to have been an essentially decent, idealistic man in whom the tragic myth of racial superiority blinded both him and others to the many other facets for good reposing in his forceful and complex personality.

We can hardly help wincing at times, however, when Dixon in his novels takes the patronizing and "superior" attitude toward the Negro. We wish then that a man of his incredible talent had directed it more completely toward constructive values. At the same time, we are reminded that Dixon was only verbally reflecting the attitudes acceptable to a major segment of American society of his time. Human nature being what it is, there is always the temptation for the critic to evaluate a figure from a past era according to the critic's own personal standards and those prevalent in his era rather than by those standards prevalent in the past. Although prejudice should not be condoned merely because it may be widespread, it is important that Dixon be understood as a spokesman for the popular tenets of his age if we are to better understand him as a man and as a writer.

The temptation of some critics is to glorify Dixon the writer on the one hand or to pillory him on the other, but yielding to such temptation may reveal the mote in the critic's eye. The conflicting reactions to Dixon's work continued after his death; and an editorial summarizing the varied careers of Dixon concluded: "There are those who would condemn the literary work of Dixon as being too inflammatory and conducive to sectional prejudice. But in stimulating the mind of the nation to think seriously upon the issues he raised in his books and in the great film whose script he wrote, Thomas Dixon indubitably contributed much to American social progress."[5]

Another critic also saw Dixon's influence as strong, but in other directions:

Thomas Dixon didn't want to start a world war. He just wanted a South in which ante-bellum chivalry could survive. He didn't want a 1920 Ku Klux Klan which would oppress Negroes, Jews, and Catholics; which would fleece its own members; which would harry organized labor; and which would set a pattern for Hitler's Nazis.

Yet his and Griffith's white-robed klansmen fired a nation's imagination to such an extent that the Latter Day K. K. K. found it a pushover sucker list when it started organizing on a grand scale.

The Klan died down in America but Hitler picked up its threads of intolerance in Germany and came within a breathless inch of weaving his dirty skein around the whole world.

None of which was the wish of Dr. Dixon. . . .[6]

III *Influence on Negro Writers*

Whatever the attitude of critics may be, they have to recognize that Dixon had a distinct influence on Negro writers in that his novels drew heavy censure from them. Charles W. Chesnutt, one of the leading Negro novelists at the turn of the twentieth century, attributed to Dixon much of the blame for discrediting the Negro in literature. After reviewing the fiction about the Reconstruction era, Chesnutt wrote: "Thomas Dixon was writing the Negro down industriously and with popular success. Thomas Nelson Page was disguising the harshness of slavery under the mask of sentiment. The trend of public sentiment at that moment was distinctly away from the Negro."[7]

In Negro fiction, we find frequent reference to the influence of Dixon's racial philosophy. J. W. Grant, in *Out of Darkness; or Diabolism and Destiny* (1909), portrayed slave trading in its worst form and the Negro at the mercy of terrorists and unscrupulous politicians during Reconstruction. Grant's novel involves three Negroes: Lucius Storms, a physician; Julius Jarnigan, a lawyer; and Harold Scott, a minister; all three men are Livingston College alumni. Storms is also a graduate of Harvard Medical School. After he discovers a cure for yellow fever, he falls in love with a white patient whose life he has saved. As soon as the white people in the vicinity learn of his love for the patient, they lynch him. In the novel, Grant writes that Southern tolerance of Dixon's racial propaganda is indicated by a newspaper reference to him: "One writer, who has done more than any

other in moulding public sentiment against the Negro, has
declared that it is his mission to drive the Negro from this
country. While we of the South know that his fabrications
are emanations from a diseased brain, yet since they help our
cause what care we?"[8]

Grant's allusion to Dixon refers to the article which Dixon
wrote for *The Saturday Evening Post* in 1905, in which he
stated that the solution to the race problem could be to colonize the American Negro in Liberia. He added that the
American government had spent about eight hundred million
dollars on Negro education since the Civil War; one-half
of the sum, he maintained, would have been sufficient to
make Liberia a powerful Negro state. In closing, Dixon
asserted that "Liberia is capable of supporting every Negro
in America. Why not face this question squarely?"[9] Like
J. W. Grant, other critics also severely criticized Dixon for
this article; and they insisted that Liberia was not large
enough to accommodate the American Negroes.

The Hindered Hand, by Sutton E. Griggs, is, however,
the most elaborate attack upon Dixon in American Negro
fiction. In this novel Griggs showed the effects of miscegenation and condemned *The Leopard's Spots* for its portrayal
of the Negro. The first and second editions of *The Hindered
Hand* (1905) contain a review of *The Leopard's Spots* in the
conversation of two of the characters; but in the third
edition of 1906 the review has been expanded into an article
at the end of the book. The article—entitled "A Hinder-
ing Hand, Supplementary to *The Hindered Hand:* A Review
of the Anti-Negro Crusade of Mr. Thomas Dixon, Jr."—states
that Dixon's malice toward the Negro derived from the traditional hatred of the Southern poor white for the Negro.
Griggs also maintains that Dixon, in his efforts to expel those
with African blood from America, attempted to discredit the
Negro, to stir up racial tension, and to send forth the Negro
burdened with obloquy and contempt. Griggs argues that
the Negro does not want to marry whites, as Dixon had maintained in the portrayal of George Harris, the young Negro
scholar, in *The Leopard's Spots*.

After his long attack, Griggs asserts that "In the long line
of men of letters of the Anglo-Saxon race we find no counter-

part to Mr. Dixon." Griggs concludes with an epitaph for the white author: "This misguided soul ignored all of the good in the aspiring Negro; made every vicious offshoot that he pictured typical of the entire race; presented all mistakes independent of their environments and provocations; ignored or minimized all the evil in the more vicious elements of whites; said and did all things which he deemed necessary to leave behind him the greatest heritage of hatred the world has ever known. Humanity claims him not as one of her children."[10]

Griggs remains as one of the most militant attackers of Dixon. As a novel, however, *The Hindered Hand* is so poorly done that much of its force is lost. The overriding purpose of the book, to counteract the work of Dixon, is so obtrusive that the reader cannot forget for a moment that the plot is a mere framework for the thesis, a feature also evident in some of Dixon's novels.

Dixon's treatment of the problem of miscegenation in *The Sins of the Father*,[11] provoked two other direct retorts in Negro fiction. One of these is *J. Johnson, or the Unknown Man: An Answer to Mr. Thos. Dixon's "Sins of the Fathers"* [*sic*], (1915) by Thomas H. B. Walker, who attempts to counteract the work of Dixon by glorifying the Negro. Johnson, the hero of the book, is a mulatto foundling who is reared by an old Negro couple. He proposes to Susan Smith, but is rejected when she learns that he is the son of a wealthy white man. Later Susan accepts Johnson when it is revealed that he is not white but of Negro-Creole extraction. Susan's early rejection of Johnson reveals Walker's brief against Dixon. The heroine maintains that the Negro has a fierce race pride which makes amalgamation unthinkable.

The other reply to Dixon is Herman Dreer's *The Immediate Jewel of His Soul* (1919) which narrates the opposition which confronts William Smith, a leading Negro exponent of the "new Negro." Smith, a graduate of several colleges in the North, accepts a pastorate at Seaton, Virginia. At a state convention of his church denomination, he strenuously urges his people to fight injustice and to seek for full political and social equality. Patience and forbearance are to be cast aside. In opposing the principles of Thomas Dixon, he says in his speech:

> Let our reproach for marriage between white and black vanish like a mist. Rather reproach the union of unequals, be they white, black or white and black. . . .
> Do not mistake that I am advocating intermarriage as a group ideal. . . . I am simply indicating the evils which arise by forbidding by law intermarriage.[12]

Because of his speech Smith is forced to relinquish his church. He starts an experimental demonstration farm to which both races are invited. Robert White, who objects to establishment of the farm, calls a meeting of the white citizens. During the meeting, one Sandy Jones attempts to arouse action against Smith by discussing Dixon's *The Clansman* and *The Birth of a Nation*: "He recalled the scene in the Southern senate, which Griffith and Dixon have made disgusting and nauseating in the extreme. He followed this with a vivid sketch of the Lieutenant-Governor's effort to force the Governor's daughter to marry him. Then he closed with praise of the Ku Klux Klan, representing it as the savior of the South. He sat down amidst great applause of half the assembly."[13]

When a mob assembles to drive Smith out of town, the concerted action of the level heads of both races averts violence. As the novel ends, Smith marries Thelma Haskell, a Negro woman who has been loyal to him throughout the upheaval. Although characterized by the exaggerations which attend the avowed propaganda novel, Dreer's work is interesting in its literary treatment of the militant Negro program for equal rights after World War I and for its direct attack on *The Clansman* which was published fourteen years before Dreer's novel.

Dixon's novels treating racial themes show a strong influence on Negro writers even into the third decade of the twentieth century. W. Forrest Cozart, in the prefatory note to *The Chosen People*, published in Boston in 1924, wrote a spirited denunciation of Dixon after reading *The Clansman* and *The Leopard's Spots*: "I then and there resolved to dedicate the rest of my life in trying to refute those false and unjust charges, and from that day until now I have been diligently working to meet those charges."[14] In Cozart's book, an extended treatment of Negroes through the ages, they are shown to be kings, prophets, inventors, and artists. The book seems to be a potential source book for current demands for "Black studies" curricula. The material, however, appears to be hastily assembled; and there seem to be glaring errors in it.

From the turn of the century until World War I, Negro writers of fiction were extremely race conscious. Although there were writers like Charles W. Chesnutt, Paul Lawrence Dunbar, John S. Durham, and George W. Ellis who generally avoided the racial problem, "a decided majority of writers answered the propaganda of Page and Dixon and sought to give the Negro a more favorable position in national opinion by glorifying him and exposing his oppressors."[15] Other Negro writers besides those already discussed reveal the influence of Dixon, for evidence of strong reaction to the racial principles in Dixon's works appears in the novels of such writers as Robert L. Waring, *As We See It* (1910); W. E. B. Dubois, *The Quest of the Silver Fleece* (1911); Yorke Jones, *The Climbers: A Story of Sun-Kissed Sweethearts* (1912); Oscar Micheaux, *The Conquest: The Story of a Negro Pioneer* (1913); William M. Ashley, *Redder Blood* (1915); and Sarah Lee Fleming, *Hope's Highway* (1918).

Dixon influenced the Negro novelist greatly. Although his influence did not encourage imitations, it motivated many writers to retaliate during the first three decades of the twentieth century. In summarizing the fiction of the Negro, until the publication of *The Leopard's Spots*, Hugh M. Gloster writes: "By praising the merits and palliating the failings of the Negro, most of these early writers proved themselves as guilty of tedium and literary distortion as were Dixon and Page. Their works are usually poor novels, because they are more polemic than fiction, and often poor polemic because they melodramatically plead the case."

With reference to the works specifically influenced by such a novelist as Dixon, Gloster concludes: "These works

. . . show the reaction of the Negro mind to the plantation tradition, Nordicism, realism, naturalism, primitivism, regionalism, proletarianism, and other significant movements in American literature. As such, this body of writing, though generally lacking the distinction that qualifies art of universal value and appeal, is an important branch of national literature describing an important aspect of national life from an important point of view."[16]

III *Dixon and Contemporary White Writers*

Among white writers Dixon's influence is less clearly assessed than it is among Negro writers of the period, for white novelists, probably affected by the popularity of his fiction, do not specifically write of Dixon or about his methods. Presumably his works gave an impetus to the writing of propaganda novels. Max Nordau, in evaluating the influence of *The Clansman*, said that "it has deliberately undone the work of Harriet Beecher Stowe."[17] The book revealed to millions of people that there was another side to Mrs. Stowe's argument; and, though this other side was biased and sensational, it gave the world at large a fuller understanding of the South's miseries after the Civil War.

An interesting influence of Dixon's Reconstruction novels is apparent in *Gone with the Wind* (1936), a later description of the South's degradation, by Margaret Mitchell. She, like Dixon, wrote one of America's best-selling novels; and she, again like Dixon, saw her work made into a famous motion picture. Moreover, she had been an eager reader of the older novelist. After she had become famous, she wrote to Dixon that she had been greatly influenced by his novels as she grew up and that she had "pirated" one of them as the basis for a play which she had presented in the family barn when she was twelve years old. The sentimental beauty and the tragedy of the Old South portrayed in Dixon's novels found expression in *Gone with the Wind,* for Miss Mitchell's work displayed the sentiment, the romance, and the Southerners' defiance that characterize Dixon's works. The struggle of human personalities in *Gone with the Wind* is reminiscent of Dixon's treatment, but the older novelist depicted these qualities somewhat more sensationally than did Miss Mitchell. Probably Dixon's strongest influence on Miss Mitchell is to be found in her portrayal of the Southerner as a proud, indomitable spirit who fights fiercely for what he holds to be right. The characters of *Gone with the Wind* are somewhat less stereotyped than those in Dixon's novels about Reconstruction, but the struggle of personalities is a marked feature of the works of both novelists.

IV *The Popular Novelist*

In Dixon's work as a popular sub-literary novelist, he suggests certain interesting comparisons with other literary figures of his own time. E. P. Roe, who, like Dixon, was a well-known minister, began his literary career as a result of his interest in a social problem. While pastor of a Presbyterian Church at Highland Falls, New York, he read in the newspapers of the great Chicago fire of 1871. He was so moved by the accounts that he immediately journeyed to Chicago, studied the troubles arising from the holocaust, and decided to write a novel based upon his experiences. *Barriers Burned Away* (1872) was immediately successful, and Roe was launched on a literary career which paid him large dividends. His literary opportunism was again revealed when he wrote *Opening a Chestnut Burr* (1874), a novel growing out of an account of the shipwreck of an ocean liner. In his novels, Roe merely exchanged the pulpit for the printed page in order to deliver his sermons to his audience.

Hall Caine, a best-selling English writer whose novels grew out of his work in the church, published *The Manxman* in 1894. His intimate friend William Rossetti had suggested to him that he use the Isle of Man as a setting for his religious novels. Dixon in a speech praised this work highly and said in answer to the "preaching" of the novel which some critics had deplored: "The marvelous power of this book is something immortal. I have never read a book of more resistless power. No man can write the truth and not preach. Talk about preaching! I try to preach, but when I read such a book I think I would crawl on my hands and knees around the world if I could write one like it. When a thousand preachers shall have died and been forgotten that book shall preach to generations yet unborn, preach to millions unchanging truths of the human heart and human life."[18]

One of the most popular of all the preacher-novelists about the turn of the century and later was Harold Bell Wright. A minister of the church of the Disciples of Christ, Wright preached a type of virile Christianity in novels that had a wide appeal for nearly three decades. Aided by a publishing friend in presenting a new novel to the public each time interest was flagging in an old one, Wright's works such as *The Shepherd of the Hills* (1907), *The Calling of Dan Matthews* (1909), and *The Winning of Barbara Worth* (1911) sold millions of copies. Several other novelists, though not ministers, should be mentioned because their best-selling novels were contemporaneous with Dixon's most popular period. The novels of such writers as Stewart Edward White, Rex Beach, James Oliver Curwood, Jack London, John Fox, Jr., and Gene Stratton-Porter were indicative of America's popular reading tastes.

In some ways Dixon fitted into this group of writers, but in others he walked a separate road. Like the other minister-novelists mentioned, Dixon carried his sermonizing into his works. His novels, like theirs, are frequently so obviously didactic in tone that the story becomes secondary to the thesis. Like the works of several of the most popular writers of the period, Dixon's novels are predominantly regional in scope. His words were gauged to reach as many readers as possible; and, as a result, his novels, like those of other popular writers of the period, rarely rise to the quality of literature. Like his contemporaries, he followed the transitory interests of the public in the various issues of the day; as these issues died, the public's interest was drawn to new areas. In many respects Dixon's novels are, therefore, typical of the popular works of his time.

But the ways in which Dixon differed from his contemporaries are worth noticing. While many of the popular novels of the period were merely entertaining, Dixon's stories of Reconstruction were highly controversial. He dealt with subjects toward which the attitudes of many readers could not be neutral, for he wrote passionately about one of the bitterest periods of human history. The subjects treated in his novels generally cover a wider range than those of the other writers mentioned, for he attempted to write about nearly every social issue of his era. Unlike most of the other popular writers, Dixon devoted only part of his strikingly varied career to writing novels. Much of his influence on American culture can also be traced to the pulpit, the lecture platform, the stage, and the motion-picture screen. Wherever the personality of the man consciously exerted itself, its force was felt by many people.

Dixon had greatly admired the works of the Polish novelist, Henryk Sienkiewicz, whose stories of oppression at the hands of conquerors suggested to Dixon a similarity between his native South and Poland. The Southerners, like the people of Poland, had suffered indignity and brutality by military occupational forces. In such novels as Sienkiewicz's *The Deluge* (1891), *By Fire and Sword* (1893), *The Children of the Soil* (1894), and *Knights of the Cross* (1899), which covers the period of the Polish struggle with the Military Order of Teutonic Knights, Dixon saw that the woes of the Polish people were in many respects like those of the Southerners during Reconstruction. Long before he began the actual writing of *The Leopard's Spots*, he had determined to write of his region in the way that Sienkiewicz had defended Poland. No other writer has dramatized the South's suffering during Reconstruction as did Dixon, and he forcefully projected in his novels the significance of that period. In his determination to inform the world of the struggles of the South, Dixon told his stories of oppression in passionate words; he heightened the colors and darkened the shadows so that his thesis stood out boldly against the background of war; and his social philosophy can best be understood in the light of his devotion to the South and to attitudes which he had learned in youth.

V *Conclusion*

Whether or not Thomas Dixon will ever be recognized as a significant figure in American literature is a question not easily dismissed. The literary quality of his novels is that of popular works that fade in importance as each generation acquires new tastes; but there can be no doubt of the sociological significance of his work. The present age is still very much concerned with the racial problems which Dixon discussed in his novels; the motion picture and its offspring, television, continue to fulfill his prophetic conviction of the unique potential of this medium; and much of the world looks apprehensively to the possibility of a Communist world state which Dixon decried so vehemently in his fiction. Many people were brought by Dixon's works and public speeches to think seriously about problems he thought of vital importance to the nation. In his own way, at times reactionary and biased, he may have tried to serve his era in a quest for better standards and ideals. There can be little doubt that Dixon's literary works have had more direct influence upon larger numbers of people than have the works of a number of "major" writers who have been acclaimed by critics but who have been read by relatively few persons in the total population.

If polarization over the issues of race and Communism increases in the future, Dixon's influence will probably become more significant than in the recent past. On the other hand, if these issues are reconciled, he will remain as an interesting, though minor, cultural phenomenon whose works expressed the attitudes of tens of millions of people at a crucial period. If indeed he is, as critics have written, "one of the greatest geniuses ever to come out of the South,"[19] and "certainly . . . the most influential literary figure ever produced by North Carolina,"[20] he will continue to draw the attention of the student of American cultural and literary history.

Notes and References

Chapter One

Occasionally sources are from clippings which do not include data beyond that listed in the notes.

1. Helen C. A. Dixon, *A. C. Dixon: A Romance of Preaching* (New York, 1931), pp. 13 and 20. LeRoy McAfee Dixon, 1853, lived only five months; Eliza Jane Dixon, 1857, lived two years; and LeRoy Dixon, 1861, who was named after the first child, "died a few months after the arrival at Little Rock." A. C. (Clarence) Dixon was born on July 6, 1854.

2. Sources, even in the Dixon family, spell Colonel McAfee's given name variously "Lee Roy," "LeRoy," and "Leroy." Since he is referred to occasionally as Lee McAfee, it is probable that the first spelling given is the one used by Colonel McAfee.

3. Thomas Dixon, "Southern Horizons: An Autobiography" (MS unfinished), p. 43.

4. *Ibid.*, p. 152.

5. *Ibid.*, p. 149.

6. *Ibid.*, p. 152.

7. *Ibid.*, p. 89.

8. *Ibid.*, p. 174.

9. In Raymond Allen Cook, *Fire From the Flint: The Amazing Careers of Thomas Dixon* (Winston-Salem, North Carolina; 1968), p. 29, Suzannah Hambright's age is erroneously given as eighty-six at the time. Inasmuch as she may have lived to be one hundred and six years old (some sources say one hundred and four), and died in 1880, she had to be about a hundred or more at the time of her journey. See Helen C. A. Dixon, p. 80.

10.. "Southern Horizons," p. 210.

11. *Ibid.*, p. 180.

12. *Ibid.*, p. 185.

Chapter Two

1. Letter dated October 6, 1882.
2. "Southern Horizons," p. 240.
3. Anon., "Chronicle and Comment," *Bookman*, XX (February, 1905), 499.
4. "Southern Horizons," p. 260.
5. *Ibid.*, pp. 260–61.
6. *Ibid.*, p. 289.
7. Mildred Louis Rutherford, *The South in History and Literature* (Atlanta, 1906), p. 605.
8. "Southern Horizons," p. 272.

Chapter Three

1. *Ibid.*, pp. 281–82.
2. Nym Crinkle [pseud. of A. C. Wheeler], "Biographical and Critical Sketch," in Thomas Dixon, *Dixon on Ingersoll: Ten Discourses Delivered in Association Hall, New York,* (New York, 1892), p. 8.
3. *The One Woman: A Story of Modern Utopia* (New York, 1903), pp. 4–5.
4. *The Life Worth Living: A Personal Experience* (New York, 1914), p. 7.
5. *Ibid.*, p. 6.
6. *The Failure of Protestantism in New York and its Causes* (New York, 1896), p. 24.
7. *Ibid.*, p. 106.
8. *Living Problems in Religion and Social Science* (New York, 1889), p. 203.
9. Mrs. Douglas Boyd, in an interview, November 16, 1951.
10. *Dixon's Sermons, Delivered in the Grand Opera House, 1898–1899* (New York, 1899), p. 88.
11. *Living Problems in Religion and Social Science*, p. 179.
12. "Try Sunday Saloons He Says," *New York Times*, February 25, 1895, p. 10.
13. *Living Problems in Religion and Social Science*, p. 173.

Chapter Four

1. "Southern Horizons," p. 377.
2. "To the Reader," p. viii.
3. "American Backgrounds for Fiction," *Bookman*, XXXVIII (January, 1914), 514.
4. *Dixon on Ingersoll*, p. 31.

5. "Censorship Means Graft Says Dixon," *New York Times*, May 15, 1924, p. 21.

6. *The Failure of Protestantism* . . . , p. 135.

7. "Southern Horizons," p. 462.

8. *Ibid.*, p. 463.

9. "Mr. Dixon's Literary Group," *New York Times*, December 31, 1894, p. 9.

10. *Living Problems in Religion and Social Science*, p. 98.

11. Quoted in Charles H. Dickey, "Thomas Dixon Born in Small N. C. Farm House," *Charlotte* (North Carolina) *Observer* May 6, 1934.

12. "Southern Horizons," p. 164.

13. R. W. Stallman, *Stephen Crane* (New York, 1968), p. 79.

14. "Southern Horizons," p. 460.

15. *Ibid.*

16. *Ibid.*, pp. 462–63.

17. *Boston Daily Herald*, April 14, 1899, n.p.

18. *Living Problems in Religion and Social Science*, p. 59.

19. *The Failure of Protestantism* . . . , p. 58.

20. *Ibid.*, pp. 58–59.

21. "Booker T. Washington and the Negro," *The Saturday Evening Post*, CLXXVIII (August 19, 1905), 2.

22. *The Leopard's Spots* (New York, 1903), p. 391.

23. *Ibid.*, p. 395.

24. *Ibid.*, p. 398.

25. "Booker T. Washington and the Negro," p. 1.

26. *The Leopard's Spots*, p. 336. For an expanded discussion of the theories mentioned, see the chapter entitled "Why the Preacher Threw His Life Away."

27. *Dixon's Sermons, Delivered in the Grand Opera House*, p. 117.

28. "Booker T. Washington and the Negro," p. 1.

29. Kelly Miller, *As to the Leopard's Spots: An Open Letter to Thomas Dixon, Jr.* (Washington, D.C., 1905), p. 19.

30. *The Failure of Protestantism* . . . , p. 115.

31. "Suburban Life for Negroes," *New York Times*, April 30, 1932, p. 14.

32. "Klan is Denounced by 'Clansman,'" *New York Times*, January 21, 1923, p. 23.

33. "Booker T. Washington and the Negro," p. 2.

34. "Facing East" (unpublished novel), p. 81.

35. *Ibid.*, p. 47.

36. "Southern Horizons," p. 102.

37. "Klan is Denounced By 'Clansman.'"

38. Quoted in David M. Chalmers, *Hooded Americanism* (Chicago, 1965), p. 93.

39. "Southern Horizons," p. 375.

40. *Ibid.*, p. 378.

41. Lilian Bell, "The Leopard's Spots," *The Saturday Evening Post*, CLXXIV (April 12, 1902), 15.

42. E. F. Harkness, *Little Pilgrimages Among the Men Who Have Written Famous Books* (Boston, 1903), p. 113.

43. "Mr. Dixon's 'The Leopard's Spots,' " *New York Times Saturday Review of Books and Art*, April 5, 1902, p. 234.

44. "The Leopard's Spots," *The Atlanta Journal*, April 20, 1902, p. 9.

45. Kelly Miller, p. 19.

46. Mansfield Allen, "Thomas Dixon's 'The Leopard's Spots,' " *Bookman*, XV (July, 1902), 472.

47. Edwin L. Shuman, "In the Realm of Books," *Chicago Record Herald*, March 15, 1902, p. 6.

48. Edwin Anderson Alderman and Joel Chandler Harris, eds., *Library of Southern Literature* (Atlanta, 1909), 1408.

49. "An Author's Answer to His Critics," *New York Times*, August 9, 1902, p. 538.

50. *Ibid.*

51. Charles Israel Landis, *Thaddeus Stevens* (Lancaster, Pennsylvania, 1916), p. 9.

52. "Mr. Dixon Makes Answer," *The Charlotte* (North Carolina) *Observer*, May 4, 1905, p. 12.

53. Edwin Anderson Alderman and Joel Chandler Harris, eds., *Library of Southern Literature*, IV, 1407.

54. Gilbert Seldes, *The Movies Come from America* (New York, 1937), p. 24.

55. *The Clansman* (New York, 1905), pp. 248–49.

56. *Ibid.*, p. 62.

57. See *The Literary Review*, July 5, 1924, p. 867; E. W. Osborn, "The Black Hood," *New York World*, June 15, 1924, p. 7; and "The Black Hood," *The* (London) *Times Literary Supplement*, August 4, 1924, p. 500.

58. Dixon never divulged the name of the woman. Could she have been Lilian Lida Bell, a popular writer who, in one of her stories, modeled Camden, a heroic minister, upon Dixon? See E. F. Harkness, *op. cit.*, pp. 127–28; and Lilian Bell's story, "Girl in Love," *Harper's Bazaar*, XXXV (November, 1903), 634.

59. "A Glance at the New Novels," *The American Monthly Review of Reviews*, XXVIII (November, 1903), 634.

60. *The Philadelphia Public Ledger,* August 17, 1903, n.p.

61. Quoted by *The National Cyclopaedia of American Biography,* XIII, 189.

62. *Dixon's Sermons,* p. 9. This sermon was delivered on Sunday, May 15, 1898, in New York City.

63. *The* (Raleigh, North Carolina) *News and Observer,* May 2, 1937, n.p.

64. Page 562.

65. Page 36.

66. *Ibid.*

67. *Ibid.,* p. 37.

68. *Ibid.*

69. "The Flaming Sword," *The* (Raleigh, North Carolina) *News and Observer,* October 23, 1937, n.p.

70. *The Flaming Sword,* p. xi.

71. Frank Smethurst, "America in Black, White, and Red," *The* (Raleigh, North Carolina) *News and Observer,* August 6, 1939, p. 5.

72. "A Novel of Conflict," *New York Times,* August 20, 1939, VI, 18.

73. *Boston Transcript,* June 14, 1916. For another unfavorable review see *New York Times,* June 18, 1916, p. 16.

74. Will Cuppy, "The Love Complex," *New York Times,* July 5, 1925, p. 12. See also *The Literary Review,* August 15, 1925, p. 3; *The Saturday Review of Literature,* II (August 29, 1925), 90; and *The New York Tribune,* July 26, 1925, p. 10.

75. *Literary Digest International Book Review,* August, 1925, p. 617.

76. "Southern Horizons," p. 317.

77. Page 288.

78. *Ibid.,* pp. 305–6.

79. Page 333.

80. "Little America," *New York Times,* August 21, 1896, p. 2.

81. From the advertisement end sheet of *The Strange Death of President Harding* (New York, 1932).

82. *A Dreamer in Portugal* (New York, 1934), p. 17.

Chapter Five

1. "Southern Horizons," p. 408.

2. *Ibid.,* p. 400.

3. Editorial, *Knoxville Journal and Tribune,* November 14, 1905, p. 4.

4. n.t., *Times Democrat* (New Orleans), December 15, 1905, p. 9.

5. n.t., *Montgomery Advertiser*, November 5, 1905, n. p.

6. *Ibid.*

7. Quoted in *Knoxville Journal and Tribune*, November 14, 1905, p. 4.

8. *Ibid.*, October 31, 1905, p. 4.

9. "Southern Horizons," p. 412.

10. *Ibid.*

11. *Ibid.*, p. 465.

12. *Ibid.*

13. Anon., *Baltimore Evening Sun*, April 3, 1946, n. p.

Chapter Six

1. Lewis Jacobs, *The Rise of the American Film: A Critical History* (New York, 1939), p. 173.

2. *The Charlotte* (North Carolina) *Observer*, October 2, 1938, n.p.

3. Jacobs, p. 179.

4. *Ibid.*, p. 174.

5. Thomas B. Gregory in the New York *American*, here quoted in *Literary Digest*, L (March, 1915), 608–9.

6. Milton Mackaye, "The Birth of a Nation," *Scribner's Magazine*, CII (November, 1937), 42.

7. "Southern Horizons," p. 424.

8. Mackaye, p. 69.

9. "Southern Horizons," p. 433.

10. Iris Barry, *D. W. Griffith, American Film Master* (New York, 1940), p. 22.

11. Quoted in "Films and Births and Censorship," *The Survey*, XXXIV (April 3, 1915), 4. See also "Censoring Motion Pictures," *New Republic*, III (June 15, 1915), 125.

12. Charlotte Rumbold, "Against 'The Birth of a Nation,' " *New Republic*, III (June 5, 1915), 125.

13. There is some difference of opinion as to whether *Gone With the Wind*, *The Birth of a Nation*, or *The Sound of Music* has earned the highest profits in the film industry. The later history of *The Birth of a Nation* is uncertain, but its foreign receipts may have made it gross more than the others. The film was distributed among numerous small companies abroad and was widely shown throughout Europe, Australia, South Africa, and South America. For discussions of the earnings of the films, see *"Quo Vadis*, Pardner?" *Time*, LXI (March 6, 1953), 108; Bosley Crowther, "Earnings of Movie at Issue," *Winston-Salem* (North Carolina) *Journal*, January 4, 1965, p. 1; Ward Greene, quoted in

Frank Veale, "Did 'The Birth of a Nation' Top 'Gone With the Wind' in Profits?" *Atlanta Times,* January 9, 1964; Charles Moore, "Biggest Money-Maker of All?" *Atlanta Constitution,* January 18, 1965, p. 12.

14. Jacobs, p. 384.

15. "Southern Horizons," p. 450.

16. The scenario for this motion picture was based in part upon Dixon's novel *The Foolish Virgin.*

17. *The Torch: The Story of a Paranoiac Who Started a Great War* (New York, 1927).

18. "Southern Horizons," p. 454.

19. *Ibid.,* p. 456.

20. *Ibid.,* pp. 456–57.

21. *Ibid.,* p. 457.

22. Edwin Anderson Alderman and Joel Chandler Harris, eds., *Library of Southern Literature* (Atlanta, 1909), IV, 1407.

Chapter Seven

1. *Wildacres: In the Land of the Sky* (Little Switzerland, North Carolina, 1926), p. 9.

2. *Ibid.,* p. 28.

3. Dedicatory page, *Living Problems in Religion and Social Science.*

4. *The* (Raleigh, North Carolina) *News and Observer,* October 13, 1936, n.p.

5. *Ibid.*

6. *Ibid.,* April 2, 1937, n.p.

7. Charles H. Dickey, "Thomas Dixon," *The Charlotte Observer,* May 6, 1934, n.p.

8. "Southern Horizons," pp. 465–66.

Chapter Eight

1. n.t. *Boston Journal,* June 17, 1902, n.p.

2. Wilson's reply to Dixon is given in Ray Stannard Baker, *Woodrow Wilson: Life and Letters,* (New York, 1937), IV, 222. The letter is dated July 29, 1913.

3. "Southern Horizons," p. 454.

4. A communication from Clara Dixon Richardson, dated January 17, 1954.

5. "Thomas Dixon" (obituary) *Winston-Salem* (North Carolina) *Journal,* April 4, 1946, n.p.

6. "Thomas Dixon", *Fayetteville* (North Carolina) *Observer,* April 4, 1946, n.p.

7. "Post-Bellum—Pre-Harlem," *Breaking into Print*, ed. Elmer Adler (New York, 1937), p. 51.

8. J. W. Grant, *Out of Darkness; or Diabolism and Destiny* (Nashville, Tennessee, 1909), p. 196.

9. "Booker T. Washington and the Negro," p. 2.

10. Sutton E. Griggs, *The Hindered Hand; or the Reign of the Repressionist* (Nashville, Tennessee, 1905), p. 2.

11. Dixon's treatment of the mulatto and of the evils arising from miscegenation was not new in fiction. Albion W. Tourgee, the Reconstruction novelist who took the Northern view, had published *Toinette* in 1876 dealing with the love of an octoroon for her former master. Two short stories of George Washington Cable, "Tite Poulette" and "Madame Delphine," are concerned with the intermarriage of the races. The problem had been further treated by such writers as Rebecca H. Davis, *Waiting for the Verdict* (1867); William Dean Howells, *An Imperative Duty* (1892); Mark Twain, *The Tragedy of Pudd'nhead Wilson* (1894); and Gertrude Atherton, *Senator North* (1907). Dixon's work is significant in that it called forth direct answers from Negro writers.

12. Herman Dreer, *The Immediate Jewel of His Soul* (St. Louis, 1919), p. 24.

13. *Ibid.*, p. 146.

14. W. Forrest Cozart, *The Chosen People* (Boston, 1924), p. 11.

15. Hugh M. Gloster, *Negro Voices in American Fiction* (Chapel Hill, North Carolina, 1948), p. 98.

16. *Ibid.*, p. 255.

17. Quoted in E. F. Harkness, p. 113.

18. *New York Times*, December 31, 1894, p. 9.

19. B.S., "Book Larning," *The State*, December 15, 1968, p. 11.

20. Charleen Whisnant, "Embarrassment of Abilities," *Winston-Salem* (North Carolina) *Journal*, January 5, 1969, n.p.

Selected Bibliography

Approximately five hundred sources have been consulted for this work. Inasmuch as no book-length study of Dixon had been published prior to this writer's, many sources, primary and secondary, were consulted which sometimes yielded only a few factual references helpful in putting together the chronology and facts of Dixon's life and careers. The following bibliography is therefore highly selective and lists only those sources which are of prime importance. For a full listing see RAYMOND ALLEN COOK, *Fire From The Flint: The Amazing Careers of Thomas Dixon.* Winston-Salem, North Carolina: John F. Blair, Publisher, 1968. In cases where only a typescript or manuscript copy of a particular work was available, no publication data are given. In a few instances the writer is not at liberty to list the source of the entry.

PRIMARY SOURCES

"The Almighty Dollar." 1912. A Play. Typescript in Library of Congress.

"American Backgrounds for Fiction." *Bookman*, XXXVIII (January, 1914), 511–14.

The Black Hood. New York: Grosset and Dunlap, 1924.

"Booker T. Washington and the Negro." *The Saturday Evening Post*, CLXXVIII (August 19, 1905), 1–2.

"The Clansman: Four Acts." 1905. Typescript in Library of Congress.

The Clansman: An Historical Romance of the Ku Klux Klan. New York: Doubleday, Page and Company, 1905.

A contract for collaborating in the writing of a drama based upon Thomas Dixon's novel *The Traitor*, November 18, 1902. Private papers of Mrs. Thomas Dixon.

Companions. New York: Otis Publishing Corporation, 1931.

Comrades. 1919. A motion picture, first entitled "Bolshevism on Trial," Library of Congress.

Comrades: A Story of Social Adventure in California. New York: Doubleday, Page and Company, 1909.

"Dangers of the Reform Administration." *New York Times,* January 21, 1895.

Dixon on Ingersoll: Ten Discourses Delivered in Association Hall, New York. New York: J. B. Alden, 1892. Step-by-step refutation of Ingersoll's views.

Dixon's Sermons, Delivered in the Grand Opera House, 1898–1899. New York: F. L. Bussey and Company, 1899.

A Dreamer in Portugal: The Story of Bernarr Macfadden's Mission to Continental Europe. New York: Covici, Friede, 1934. Enthusiastic portrayal of the physical culture goals of Macfadden.

"The Drift Toward Anarchy." *New York Times,* October 5, 1896, p. 5.

The Failure of Protestantism in New York and its Causes. New York: V. O. A. Strauss, 1896.

The Fall of a Nation: A sequel to the Birth of a Nation. New York: D. Appleton and Company, 1916.

The Flaming Sword. Atlanta: Monarch Publishing Company, 1939.

The Foolish Virgin: A Romance of Today. New York: D. Appleton and Company, 1915.

"Frank Dixon: A Sketch by His Brother." A clipping from a North Carolina newspaper, n.d., n.p.

"From the Horrors of City Life." *World's Work,* IV (October, 1902), 2603–11.

The Hope of the World: A Story of the Coming War. New York: [The author], 1925.

The Inside Story of the Harding Tragedy. New York: The Churchill Company, 1932.

A letter to Louise Dixon, postmarked September 8, n.d., commemorating her birthday.

Letters to Henry Cathcart, October 29, 1901; October 30, 1902; July 17, 1903; and February 20, 1905. Emory University Library. Interesting correspondence concerning publishing matters.

A contract to sell the motion picture rights of Thomas Dixon's novel *The Way of a Man,* September 12, 1919.

The Leopard's Spots: A Romance of the White Man's Burden. New York: Doubleday, Page and Company, 1903.

"The Leopard's Spots." Independent, LVII (November 7, 1904), 1149.

The Life Worth Living: A Personal Experience. New York: Doubleday, Page and Company, 1914. Interesting glimpses of Dixon's family life at Elmington Manor, Dixondale, Virginia.

Living Problems in Religion and Social Science. New York: C. T. Dillingham, 1889.

The Love Complex. New York: Boni and Liveright, 1925.

The Man in Gray: A Romance of North and South. New York: D. Appleton and Company, 1921.

A Man of the People: A Drama of Abraham Lincoln. New York: D. Appleton and Company, 1920.

The Mark of the Beast, 1923. A motion picture by Dixon Studios. Typescript in Library of Congress.

"The Moral Import of the News," a radio broadcast over station WJZ, New York, by invitation of the National Broadcasting Company, October 2, 1933.

"The Negro and the South." *Christian Union,* XLIII (May 22, 1890), 39.

Old Black Joe, 1912. A play. Typescript in Library of Congress.

The One Woman: A Drama. New York: Munn and Company, 1906.

The One Woman: A Story of Modern Utopia. New York: Doubleday, Page and Company, 1903.

"Political Equality." A pamphlet. New York: [The author], n.d. Private papers of Mrs. Thomas Dixon.

"The Red Dawn: A Drama of Revolution." 1919. Typescript copy in Library of Congress.

"A Reply to [Howard] Scott's Speech on Technocracy." A speech delivered before the Kappa Alpha Fraternity at the Hotel Shelton, New York City, January 19, 1933, in celebration of the birthday of Robert E. Lee. Private papers of Mrs. Thomas Dixon.

The Root of Evil: A Novel. Garden City, New York: Doubleday, Page and Company, 1911.

The Sins of the Father: A Romance of the South. New York: D. Appleton and Company, 1912.

The Southerner: A Romance of the Real Lincoln. New York: Grosset and Dunlap, 1913.

"Southern Horizons: An Autobiography." An unpublished manuscript. Indispensable for knowledge of Dixon's early life and many of his personal opinions about literature and public matters. From the private papers of Mrs. Thomas Dixon.

The Sun Virgin. New York: Horace Liveright, 1929.

The Torch: A Story of the Paranoiac Who Caused a Great War. A motion picture scenario. New York [The author], 1927.

The Traitor: A Story of the Fall of the Invisible Empire. New York: Doubleday, Page and Company, 1907.
The Victim: A Romance of the Real Jefferson Davis. New York: Grosset and Dunlap, 1914.
The Way of a Man: A Story of the New Woman. New York: D. Appleton and Company, 1912.
What is Religion? An Outline of Vital Ritualism. New York: The Scott Publishing Company, 1891.
Wildacres: In the Land of the Sky. Little Switzerland, North Carolina: The Mount Mitchell Association of Arts and Sciences, 1926.
"Young Men of New York," *Harper's Weekly,* XXXV (August 29, 1891), 652.

SECONDARY SOURCES

The following sources are highly selective. For an extensive bibliography, consult Cook, Raymond A., *Fire From the Flint,* listed below.

ADAMS, HERBERT B. "Bibliography of Thomas Dixon." Unpublished bibliography. Johns Hopkins University Library, 1902. Helpful but by no means extensive; deals only with Dixon's early career.
Addresses, Letters and Papers of Clyde Roark Hoey, Governor of North Carolina 1937-1941. Ed. DAVID LEROY CORBITT. Raleigh: Council of State, State of North Carolina, 1944. Interesting glimpses of Dixon's North Carolina and times.
ALLEN, JAMES STEWART. *Reconstruction: The Battle for Democracy.* New York: International Publishers, 1937. Useful for understanding the time of Dixon's boyhood in the South.
ASHE, SAMUEL. *A Court Biographical History of North Carolina.* Chapel Hill: University of North Carolina, 1908. Interesting information concerning Dixon's political life.
Atlanta *Constitution,* "The Clansman," October 16, 1905, October 31, 1905. Interesting reactions to Dixon's play.
BARDECHE, MAURICE AND ROBERT BRASILLACH. *The History of Motion Pictures.* Translated and edited by Iris Barry. New York: W. W. Norton Company and The Museum of Modern Art, 1938. Both this source and the one following are invaluable for the understanding of the status of motion pictures at the time *The Birth of a Nation* was filmed.

BARRY, IRIS. *D. W. Griffith, American Film Master.* New York: The Museum of Modern Art, 1940. Excellent study of the director of *The Birth of a Nation.*

BELL, LILIAN LIDA. "A Collarless Novelist," *Saturday Evening Post,* CLXXIV (May 3, 1903), 17. This article and the two following seem to express more than academic interest in Dixon the man.

———. "Girl in Love." *Harper's Bazaar,* XXV (November, 1901), 603–8.

———. "The Leopard's Spots." *Saturday Evening Post,* CLXXIV (April 12, 1908), 15.

The Booker T. Washington Collection, Library of Congress, Washington, D. C. Extremely valuable collection; indispensable to a study of the Dixon-Washington relationship or controversy.

COOK, RAYMOND A. *Fire From the Flint.* Winston-Salem, North Carolina: John F. Blair, 1968. First biography of Dixon. Contains an extensive bibliography.

———. "The Versatile Career of Thomas Dixon." *Emory University Quarterly,* XI (June, 1955), 103–12. Concise view of Dixon the man and novelist.

———. "The Literary Principles of Thomas Dixon." *The Georgia Review,* XIII (Spring, 1959), 97–102. Dixon explains his literary credo.

———. "The Man Behind The Birth of a Nation." *The North Carolina Historical Review,* XXXIX (October, 1962), 519–40. Fairly extensive account of Dixon's relation to the motion-picture industry.

COULTER, E. MERTON. *The South During Reconstruction 1865–1877.* Baton Rouge, Louisiana: Louisiana State University Press, 1947. Authoritative from the more traditional view of the effects of Reconstruction.

DAPONTE, DURANT. "The Greatest Play of the South." *Tennessee Studies in Literature,* II (1957), 13–20. Excellent recounting of the history of Dixon's play *The Clansman.* Professor DaPonte used extensively the Booker T. Washington Collection of the Library of Congress.

DIXON, HELEN C. A. *A. C. Dixon: A Romance of Preaching.* New York: G. P. Putnam's Sons, 1931. Biography of Dixon's brother; though a work of enthusiasm for the author's husband, it is very helpful in establishing the chronology of the Dixon family.

"The Dixon Collection." Historical Commission of the Southern Baptist Convention. Nashville, Tennessee. Extensive and indispensable sources on the Dixon family, particularly A. C. Dixon.

DU BOIS, W. E. BURGHARDT. *Black Reconstruction* New York: Harcourt, Brace and Company, 1935. Reconstruction from the viewpoint of the Black man. Emotional.

GLOSTER, HUGH M. *Negro Voices in American Fiction.* Chapel Hill: The University of North Carolina Press, 1948. Indispensable for revealing the racial attitudes in some Negro writers. Well-balanced study.

GRIGGS, SUTTON E. *The Hindered Hand; or the Reign of the Repressionist.* 3rd ed. rev. Nashville, Tennessee: The Orion Publishing Company, 1905. Full-length attack in fiction upon Dixon and his novels dealing with the Negro.

HARRIS, MAX FRANK. "The Ideas of Thomas Dixon on Race Relations." Unpublished master's thesis, University of North Carolina, 1948. Helpful; sometimes inexact in reference and facts.

HORN, STANLEY F. *Invisible Empire: The Story of the Ku Klux Klan 1866–1871.* Boston: Houghton Mifflin Company, 1939. Basic study of the genesis and influence of the Klan.

LUTZ, SISTER M. ANGELITA. "Thomas Dixon's Contribution to American Literature with Special Reference to the Original Manuscript of *The Root of Evil.*" Unpublished master's thesis, Saint Bonaventure College, 1948. Title far more ambitious than the thesis proves to be.

MACKAYE, MILTON. "The Birth of a Nation." *Scribner's Magazine,* CII (November, 1937), 40–46. Valuable for background on some aspects of the film.

New York Times. The following entries from the *Times* are indispensable for nearly every aspect of Dixon's public life. No serious research on Dixon could be pursued without these valuable sources. Dixon was in the news frequently over a period of years, and the *New York Times* was a repository for many of his pronouncements, speeches, and debates.

1895

"Try Sunday Saloons He Says," February 25, p. 10; "Savannah Officials Condemned," March 4, p. 11; "Rev. Thomas Dixon Resigns," March 11, p. 8; "Dixon's Church the People's," March 18, p. 2; "Sunday Was Not So Dry," July 15, p. 1; "Would Like to Be a Hornet," October 29, p. 14.

1896
"Put Out for Changing His Seat," September 21, p. 2.

1897
"The Rev. Dixon's New Boat," December 6, p. 2.

1899
"Thomas Dixon, Jr., Resigns," January 16, p. 10.

1903
"The Negro a Menace Says Thomas Dixon," June 9, p. 2.

1906
"Hot Talk in Church After Dixon Spoke," January 29, p. 4.

1915
"The Birth of a Nation," March 4, p. 9; "Negroes Object to Film," March 7, p. 13; "A Woman's Protest," March 21, III, p. 2; "Protests on Photo Play," March 31, p. 9; "Conference on Moving Pictures," April 2, p. 13; "Egg Negro Scenes in Liberty Film Play," April 15, p. 1; "Negroes Mob Photo Play," April 18, II, p. 15; "Ban on Film Play Lifted," August 15, II, p. 13; "Refuses to Enjoin Epoch Company," September 1, p. 9.

1916

"Suit Over Big Film Play," January 29, p. 10; "Herbert Writes For Film," May 3, p. 11; "A Ku Klux Statue," September 26, p. 10; "In Favor of a Kuklux Statue," September 28, p. 8; "Against a Kuklux Statue," September 30, p. 10.

1922
"Walker and Chase Tilt on Movies," February 22, p. 17.

1923
"Klan Is Denounced By 'The Clansman,' " January 23, p. 23; "Klokard Haywood Here to Aid Ku Klux," February 5, p. 4; "Mark of the Beast," June 2, p. 14.

1924
"Censorship Means Graft, Says Dixon," May 15, p. 21; "Dixon Condemns Klan," August 5, p. 18.

1928
"Dixon Files $500,000 Suit," February 25, p. 2.

1931
"Dixon Urges Cut in Price of Books," February 11, p. 9.

1932
"Suburban Life for Negroes," April 30, p. 14.

1933
"Scores Dr. Butler Over Technocracy," January 20, p. 5.

1934
"Dixon Penniless; $1,250,000 Gone," April 17, p. 19.

1936

"Sharp Attack at Macon," January 30, p. 1; "Rally for Talmadge Leaves Some Doubts," February 2, IV, p. 5; "Dixon to Stump for Landon," September 9, p. 19.

1937
"Thomas Dixon in Court Job," May 2, II, p. 10.

1946
"Thomas Dixon Dies; Wrote 'Clansman'," April 4, p. 25.

OAKES, FRANCES. "Whitman and Dixon: A Strange Case of Borrowing." *The Georgia Review*, XI (Fall, 1957), 333—40. Professor Oakes discusses Dixon's plagiarism of material from Walt Whitman.

Raleigh *News and Observer*, October 1, 1905. This entry and those following from the *News and Observer* are valuable for appraisals of a "native son." These entries are from clippings, and no data are available other than the following dates: October 13, 1936; May 2, 1937; October 22, 1937; March 21, 1939; May 31, 1940; July 3, 1943; April 4, 1946.

WEATHERS, LEE B. *Thomas Dixon: North Carolina's Most Colorful Character of his Generation—Lawyer, Minister, Author, Orator, Playwright, Actor.* Shelby, North Carolina: [The author], 1949. Valuable for personal reminiscences of a home-town friend.

Index

Index